BRIGHT I

THE IDIOT
BY
FYODOR
DOSTOYEVSKY

Intelligent Education

INFLUENCE PUBLISHERS

Nashville, Tennessee

BRIGHT NOTES: The Idiot

www.BrightNotes.com

ISBN: 978-1-645421-42-9 (Paperback)
ISBN: 978-1-645421-43-6 (eBook)

Published in accordance with the U.S. Copyright Office Orphan Works and Mass Digitization report of the register of copyrights, June 2015.

Originally published by Monarch Press.
David A. Gooding, 1965
2019 Edition published by Influence Publishers.

Interior design by Lapiz Digital Services. Cover Design by Thinkpen Designs.

Printed in the United States of America.

Library of Congress Cataloging-in-Publication Data forthcoming.
Names: Intelligent Education
Title: BRIGHT NOTES: The Idiot
Subject: STU004000 STUDY AIDS / Book Notes

CONTENTS

INTRODUCTION TO FYODOR DOSTOYEVSKY

BIOGRAPHICAL SKETCH OF DOSTOYEVSKY

Fyodor Mikhailovich Dostoyevsky was born October 30, 1821, in Moscow, the second son of Mikhail, a physician at the Mariinsky Hospital for the Poor. The family belonged to the hereditary nobility and possessed a small country estate worked by some one hundred "souls" as serfs were then called. Late every spring the family left Moscow to spend the summer there.

After Fyodor completed his secondary education, his father sent him in 1838 to St. Petersburg where he entered the College of Engineers, a military school run by the Czar. Although he studied hard and in general made a good impression on his teachers, the young cadet was in constant financial straits. Always writing home for more money, he describes his "terrible plight" in the most urgent terms. When money came, though, he celebrated its arrival with a huge banquet and drinking party for his friends, or gambled it away shooting pool. He was generous to the point of self-destruction. When his brother Mikhail was married, Fyodor sent him one hundred fifty rubles. Two weeks later he was broke again, begging him for five. This inability to manage his finances persisted throughout his life. In fact, he was nearly always on the brink of bankruptcy.

Despite his ups and downs in Petersburg, the twenty-three-year-old Dostoyevsky became so attached to the city that the mere thought of living elsewhere was unbearable for him. So when he learned that he was about to be posted to the provinces, he resigned his commission and resolved to support himself by writing. In 1846 *Poor Folk* was published and immediately became a best seller. The young author was lionized as the new Gogol, received into the best houses, and became the object of unrestrained praise. The novel is a brilliantly written though sentimental story about the destructive effects of poverty. In quick succession there followed *The Double* (1846) and a collection of short stories under the title *White Nights* (1848).

About this time Dostoyevsky became seriously ill, both mentally and physically. Poor, quarrelsome, the victim of unpredictable fevers and convulsions, he soon alienated his admirers as well as his editors. Furthermore, since his erratic behavior was put down to personality rather than to the illness that it was, he was frequently laughed at, jeered, and mocked. Turgenev, for instance, so despised him that he would engage him in conversation merely for the pleasure of torturing him. Still, Dostoyevsky was reckoned among the most promising young writers of the day. Unfortunately, his literary career was suddenly interrupted by a remarkable incident that was the direct consequence of his political involvement.

SENTENCED TO DEATH

Ever since the Decembrist revolt in 1825 it had become fashionable for men of learning to promote social reform. Revolutionary manifestoes were printed abroad, smuggled into the country, and widely distributed. Czar Nicholas I, however, was determined that there would be no revolution in Russia under him. Censorship was severe and many domestic and foreign authors were banned. The penalties for revolutionary activity were increased, and government spies were everywhere. Notwithstanding, Dostoyevsky joint a group of political rebels who met ever Friday evening at Mikhail Petrashevsky's apartment. Here they discussed different political trends, plotting revolution on the side in a rather harmless way. All the same, the government became suspicious. The members of the circle were arrested, brought to trial, and Dostoyevsky, along with several others, was sentenced to death.

Finally, on a cold winter morning after a miserable stay in prison, the future author and his co-conspirators were driven to their place of execution. There, tied to stakes, the unlucky men faced the firing squad. However, as the soldiers were given the order to aim, a horseman suddenly appeared riding full tilt across the square. He bore a letter from the Czar commuting all the death sentences to prison terms. The entire affair was prearranged to frighten them and others of their kind into submission to the Czarist regime.

"TO LIVE, NO MATTER HOW"

Needless to say, Dostoyevsky was profoundly affected by this brief encounter with death. So much so in fact that the **theme** of the condemned man appears on countless occasions in his letters, articles, and novels. Among the most forceful passages describing the condemned man's state of mind occurs in *Crime and Punishment* when Raskolnikov says: "Someone condemned to death thinks an hour before his death that if he had to live on a steep pinnacle or on a rock or on a cliff edge so narrow that there was only room to stand, and around him there were abysses, the ocean, and everlasting darkness, eternal solitude, eternal tempests - if he had to remain standing on a few square inches of space for a thousand years or all eternity, it would be better to live than to die. Only to live, to live, to live, no matter how."

Dostoyevsky's will to live was severely tested by the Czar's verdict. He was sentenced to four years' hard labor in Siberia followed by another five as a common soldier in a penal battalion. The years of physical hardship, loneliness, and the study of the Bible, the only reading allowed the prisoners, completely changed the author's way of thinking. In both religion and politics he turns into an outspoken conservative, a staunch supporter of the Czarist regime, and the Russian Orthodox Church. He becomes convinced that an Orthodox Christian will, of his own accord, subject himself joyfully to the will of God. Furthermore, by some mystic fiat, a true Russian's political strivings will miraculously coincide with the will of the Czar Emancipator. These attitudes form the basis of Dostoyevsky's dialectical thought and ultimately determine whether his heroes are saved or destroyed.

Thus when in 1859, ten years after his arrest, Dostoyevsky is permitted to resign from the army and return to Petersburg, we meet a changed writer, but not a less productive one. Shortly after his release he publishes an account of his imprisonment, *Notes from the House of the Dead* (1860). This is followed by the short novel *The Insulted and the Injured* (1861). He even tries his hand at journalism, successfully editing his own paper. Unfortunately, his troubles with the regime are not over. His journal, *Vremya*, is considered subversive and ordered closed. Disgusted, Dostoyevsky decides to leave Russia for Europe.

In Wiesbaden he won a large sum of money which allowed him the luxury of an affair with the beautiful, charming, and intelligent Polina Suslova. They toured Europe together visiting all the "in" places until he lost his money. Possessing a destructive passion for gambling, he could not keep away from the casinos. On several occasions he lost everything and had to write friends in Russia for the fare home.

The novel *The Gambler* (1866) is a thinly veiled autobiographical account of this trip. The book is also the third major work in the most productive period of his life which begins in 1864 with the publication of *Notes from Underground*. During the next sixteen years Dostoyevsky worked feverishly, producing among other things five major novels and *The Diary of a Writer*. In addition, he maintained a voluminous correspondence with friends, acquaintances, and various admirers who wrote for advice.

MARRIAGE AND FAME

Dostoyevsky's existence changed for the better with his marriage to Anna Snitkina, his secretary. Among her many qualities was a good business sense that enabled her to offset her husband's inability to manage his finances. There were trips abroad and every summer the family rented a small cottage in the country. Dostoyevsky could now truly enjoy his fame as one of Russia's leading authors and was finally able to write at his leisure.

Yet Dostoyevsky's health was always bad. Since his return from Siberia he suffered from epilepsy and these attacks increased with alarming frequency in the 1860s. During the worst period the fits came once a month and so exhausted him that he needed several days to recover. In addition, he contracted tuberculosis in the 1870s which, together with lung cancer, precipitated his death January 28, 1881.

ST. PETERSBURG: DOSTOYEVSKY'S BAD DREAM

The background of many of the author's stories, Dostoyevsky's St. Petersburg seems to be a flat, featureless wasteland. Its buildings lack character and its streets are dismal alleyways rarely touched by daylight. To Dostoyevsky, St. Petersburg seemed often so unreal that he was haunted by the prospect that it was simply someone's dream and that upon awakening everything would disappear leaving only the marshes and lakes. Others had felt likewise before him. When Peter the Great realized his ambition to build a city upon the Finnish marsh, the peasants living in the vicinity thought that it had been pulled down from the sky. It is only fitting that in such a city human activity is subdued. There is no hustle and bustle in Dostoyevsky's city streets, nor do we find the comforting noise of people going about their daily business. Rarely anything takes place in open daylight. The city seems to be condemned to perpetual twilight through which Dostoyevsky's characters hurry to their non-descript lodgings.

Thus, Dostoyevsky never describes a city in the manner of Balzac. In fact, he had an antipathy toward any kind of description of buildings or landscapes, saying that he had better things to do than waste time over creating word pictures. Consequently, he draws the barest outlines and leaves the reader to fill in the details. From another angle, this method is all the more effective because it allows the reader to create his own image of the city.

We could say that the author conceives St. Petersburg like a map. He chooses a location and then strictly adheres to its dimensions. In *Crime and Punishment*, for example, we know exactly where Raskolnikov lives, how many paces to the moneylender's house, and how far it is to the police station. Often Dostoyevsky's favorite places are the ones he personally knows. Central to *Crime and Punishment* is Haymarket Square close to which the author lived for many years. An unbelievably filthy quarter, it is the gathering place of thieves, prostitutes and the like. Surrounding the square are the stalls from which are hawked all manner of merchandise of use only to the destitute. Leading off the square are trash-filled alleyways bordered by pothouses and bodakings of the worst kind. Like Raskolnikov, Dostoyevsky loved to wander aimlessly about the place filling his lungs with the fetid air as if he were inhaling the essence of being. Still, precise descriptions of the place are absent. The scenery resembles a rather hastily erected stage set. Yet, we sense it as real because the characters are real, often uncomfortably so.

THE IDIOT

CHARACTER OF PRINCE MYSHKIN

In letters written to friends and relatives at the time, Dostoyevsky stated that *The Idiot* was to be the portrait of a "perfect man." Prince Myshkin (who is called an "idiot" because his epileptic condition was thought to have resulted in mental illness at one time) is a simple, painfully honest and completely good person. He is unable to believe that anyone is bad; even when he realizes that someone wishes him harm, he forgives his "enemy" and feels that he himself must be at fault. In other words, he possesses that rarest of Christian virtues, true humility. There are numerous indications in the novel that Prince Myshkin is a Christ-figure. Indeed, Dostoyevsky's notes for the novel indicate that the Prince is to represent Christ. Unfortunately for the Prince, his Christian virtues have no place in the real world; he is laughed at, and his efforts to help the various people whom he meets are unsuccessful.

PLOT

It is difficult to summarize the plot of *The Idiot* in a few words, but briefly, the core of the novel concerns the Prince's relationships with three people: Nastasya Filippovna, a "fallen woman"; Aglaia Epanchin, a "pure" and wholesome girl of good family; and Rogozhin, a fairly wealthy young man who is the Prince's opposite and his antagonist. The Prince loves both of these women, but his love is Christian, rather than sexual. He offers to marry Nastasya, because he pities her, but she laughs at him and runs off with Rogozhin. Eventually Nastasya returns and forces the Prince to choose between her and Aglaia. Prince Myshkin chooses Nastasya, again because he pities her. But just before their marriage is to take place, on the very steps of the church, Nastasya sees Rogozhin in the crowd and runs away with him. The Prince follows them to St. Petersburg, meets Rogozhin, and together they keep watch over Nastasya, whom Rogozhin had murdered, as the Prince had long feared he would.

FAILURE OF PRINCE MYSHKIN

Prince Myshkin's attempts to practice Christian love and humility failed because the real world in which he found himself was unable to accept his love. In many ways, *The Idiot* foreshadows "The Legend of the Grand Inquisitor" in *The Brothers Karamazov*, where Christ, returning to the world during the time of the Inquisition in Spain, is arrested by the Grand Inquisitor and told that his teachings are dangerous and unsuitable for mankind. Just as Christ is told by the Grand Inquisitor to "go and come no more," Prince Myshkin is utterly defeated and must return to the Swiss sanitarium in which he had spent his youth. *The Idiot* also reminds us of *Don Quixote*, Cervantes' picaresque novel about a would-be knight in an age no longer chivalrous. Prince Myshkin, a Christian in a materialistic world, is just as out of place as *Don Quixote*.

MYSHKIN VERSUS ROGOZHIN

In Dostoyevsky's first notes for *The Idiot*, the "idiot" was a character having both sublime good and diabolical evil contained in him. Eventually, the character became two, Prince Myshkin and Rogozhin. Dostoyevsky's interest in the "split personality" (of the Dr. Jekyl and Mr. Hyde type, although much more subtly drawn) had been evident in earlier works (for instance, *The Double*, which was written in 1846), and continued to preoccupy him during the remainder of his life.

"THE LIFE OF A GREAT SINNER"

Dostoyevsky had long planned to write an **epic** composed of five novels, to be called collectively, "*The Life of Great Sinner*." It was to be the chronicle of an evil man, beginning with his youth, who yet had enough good in him to end his life as a sincere penitent. The work, for which Dostoyevsky made only a few preliminary notes, would have been largely autobiographical and would have reiterated the **theme** of the "double" man. Dostoyevsky as not a "great sinner," but he felt that he might have become one.

THE BROTHERS KARAMAZOV

Some of his ideas for "The Life of a Great Sinner" were incorporated in *The Idiot* and in *The Possessed*. Dostoyevsky's last two novels, *A Raw Youth* which appeared in 1875, and *The Brothers Karamazov* which was completed at the end of 1880, follow the general scheme of "The Life of a Great Sinner." Letters written at the time *The Brothers Karamazov* was finished indicate that Dostoyevsky intended to write a sequel to it, but he left no preliminary sketches for the work.

THE DIARY OF A WRITER

After his return to Russia in 1871, Dostoyevsky supported his family by contributing to various periodicals, one of which he edited for a short time. His articles appeared under the general title, *The Diary of a Writer*, and ranged from reminiscences of his early years to short stories to pronouncements of his political and social beliefs. He was now famous and financially secure. Less than a year before his death, Dostoyevsky scored his greatest triumph when, at a Pushkin festival in Moscow (celebrating the forty-third anniversary of the death of the great Russian poet), he electrified the audience by preaching the new brotherhood of all men.

DOSTOYEVSKY'S DEATH

Dostoyevsky's health had never been good and he continued to suffer from the epileptic seizures which had begun in Siberia. He was also plagued by a lung condition which became steadily worse and ultimately caused his death on January 28, 1881. All St. Petersburg mourned him, and the State, which had once nearly executed him, offered to pay for his funeral.

THE IDIOT

PART I

PART I, CHAPTER 1

Three men meet in a third class compartment of the train from Warsaw to St. Petersburg. It is November and cold. Evidently one of the men is a stranger to Russian weather, for he is not warmly enough dressed. The appearance of two of the men is described in some detail. One, whom we later learn is Parfyon Semyonovitch Rogozhin, is described as looking as though he had just recovered from an illness. His smile is insolent, his expression is conceited, but he also has a passionate look about him. The other, who soon introduces himself as Price Lyov Nikolayevich Myshkin, is described as having a strange look which some can recognize as belonging to those who suffer from epilepsy.

Prince Myshkin is evidently naive and friendly, answering all questions, no matter how rude, without taking offense. He tells Rogozhin that he has been in Switzerland for four years, under medical treatment for epilepsy, and that his patron, a man named

Pavlishtchev, had died without providing for him. Myshkin says that he is improved, but not cured. He has no money, and knows no one in Russia. However, he has a distant relation in St. Petersburg, Madame Epanchin, whom he hopes to meet.

At this point, the third man in the carriage, who does not introduce himself, but who refers to himself as Lebedyev, enters the conversation. He seems to know "everything" and is quite eager to show off his knowledge of the various people mentioned.

Comment: In describing the appearances of Myshkin and Rogozhin, the author has told us more about their characters than about their physical appearances. Rogozhin is "passionate" while Myshkin is a "dreamer." Dostoyevsky's concern with character indicates that *The Idiot* is more a psychological novel than a purely narrative novel.

Lebedyev is not described. However, in an "aside," Dostoyevsky tells us about people of Lebedyev's type. They are generally minor officials, who are paid very little and who delight in knowing about important people. They know who the important people are related to, how much money they have, what scandals they are involved in, and things of that nature. However, people like Lebedyev are rarely, if ever, acquainted with the important people they talk about.

Dostoyevsky's way of introducing these three men indicates that Rogozhin and Myshkin will be important characters in the novel and that Lebedyev will not.

By the time the train arrives in St. Petersburg, we know that Rogozhin's father died recently and that Rogozhin will inherit a large fortune. We also hear, for the first time, of Nastasya Filippovna Barashkov, over whom Rogozhin has quarreled with his father. She has apparently been living with Afanasy Ivanovitch Totsky, a man twice her age. She is very beautiful and rather unapproachable.

Rogozhin tells Prince Myshkin, as the train reaches its destination, that he will provide him with money and warm clothes that evening. Rogozhin goes off with a crowd of friends who have come to meet him, and Lebedyev follows. Prince Myshkin sets out to visit the Epanchins.

Comment: The first chapter "sets the scene" and introduces the following characters:

1) **Prince Myshkin, an epileptic, who is returning to Russia after four years in Switzerland.**

2) **Rogozhin, who is about to inherit a large sum of money and who is in love with Nastasya Filippovna.**

3) **Lebedyev, a minor government official, who will attach himself to anyone rich or important.**

PART I, CHAPTER 2

Prince Myshkin calls at the home of General Ivan Fyodorovitch Epanchin, whose wife, the former Princess Myshkin, is a distant relative of the Prince's. Myshkin is very friendly and shocks the footman by talking to him. Somehow, the conversation touches on capital punishment, and Prince Myshkin describes an execution he recently witnessed in France. He says that judicial execution is worse for the victim than criminal murder, because a condemned man knows that his life will not be saved at the last minute.

> **Comment: In Prince Myshkin's impassioned statement concerning the feelings of a condemned man, Dostoyevsky is obviously giving his own opinion, based on his own experience. He also indicates that he is against capital punishment by referring to it as judicial murder. Prince Myshkin wonders what it must feel like, to be condemned to death, and states that perhaps someone who had been reprieved at the last moment could tell him. We know that Dostoyevsky is referring to himself as the reprieved man.**

General Epanchin is described as a self-made man who, although possessing considerable intelligence, prefers to let it appear that he only carries out the orders of others. Madame Epanchin, proud of her birth, has a number of influential friends. The Epanchins have three daughters, Alexandra, Adelaida and Aglaia, all of whom are attractive, intelligent, well-educated and talented. However, none of them is married yet.

The General's secretary, Gavril Ardalionovitch Ivolgin (we learn his last name later), remembers that the Prince had written to Madame Epanchin sometime before and shows the Prince into the General's office.

> **Comment: This chapter leads up to an important event: Prince Myshkin's meeting with the Epanchin family. We also learn more about the Prince's character.**

PART I, CHAPTER 3

Prince Myshkin meets General Epanchin and tells him that the entire object of his visit is to make his acquaintance. He says that even if he were invited to stay with the Epanchin, family, he would refuse to do so; that he has a certain business affair to discuss with the General; and that he hopes to find some kind of work.

Comment: We do not learn until much later that the Prince's "business" concerns a legacy left to him.

Prince Myshkin readily answers the questions General Epanchin fires at him and is not offended, even though the General is quite rude at times. Finally, the General is disarmed by Myshkin's obvious sincerity and friendliness, and offers to help him obtain a job.

The Prince demonstrates his only talent, excellent handwriting. While he is doing this, the General and Gavril Ardalionovitch, who is called Ganya, talk about Nastasya Filippovna, whose birthday it is. She has given Ganya a picture of herself. It appears that Ganya has asked her to marry him and that she will answer him that evening. From the conversation, it is evident that Ganya's mother does not approve of the match.

Comment: The following chapter will inform us of the circumstances surrounding Nastasya Filippovna and Ganya.

Prince Myshkin looks at Nastasya's portrait and remarks on how beautiful she is. He tells Ganya and the General of his conversation with Rogozhin that morning, in which he first heard of Nastasya.

Comment: It seems odd that the General and Ganya should discuss to private a matter as Ganya's relations with Nastasya in front of the Prince, After all, he is a complete stranger to them. By having them do this, Dostoyevsky has again enlarged our understanding of Myshkin's character: he seems so naive that people, for example Ganya and the General, feel that they can talk freely before him, just as they would if he were a child.

After showing off his examples of calligraphy with child-like pride and enthusiasm, the Prince is promised a job by the general. General Epanchin then advises the Prince to stay at Ganya's home instead of at a hotel. He states that Ganya's mother rents out rooms to "selected" lodgers.

Comment: We learn later that the only lodger Nina Alexandrovna Ivolgin, Ganya's mother, has is a man named Ferdyshtchenko, to whom the General makes an unfavorable reference. It is apparent that Ganya and his family are rather poor.

The General then goes off to see if his wife, Lizaveta Prokofyena, wishes to see the Prince. Ganya takes this opportunity to ask Prince Myshkin his opinion of Nastasya and of Rogozhin.

Comment: Although Ganya apparently is not very eager to marry Nastasya (there is also his mother's opposition to consider), he seems worried about the threat of competition which Rogozhin represents.

Prince Myshkin tells Ganya that he admires Nastasya greatly, fees that she has suffered, and wonders whether she is kindhearted. However, he says that he could not marry her, or anyone, because he is an invalid. He goes on to say that while Rogozhin might marry Nastasya "tomorrow," he is also capable of murdering her. Ganya becomes very upset at these words, but the Prince does not have time to ask him what is wrong, because at that moment he is given a message that Madame Epanchin wishes to see him.

Comment: Having a kind heart is a redeeming feature, as far as the Prince is concerned. In this chapter he says that it makes all the difference in the world, and he acts according to this creed throughout the novel.

Although Prince Myshkin declares his inability to marry, later that evening he does offer to marry Nastasya.

Prince Myshkin's statement that Rogozhin might murder Nastasya is clearly prophetic. Dostoyevsky thus shows that Prince Myshkin, although he himself declares that he was once so ill as to be almost an "idiot," is an excellent judge of character.

PART I, CHAPTER 4

Comment: This chapter represents a digression on the part of the novelist, who takes this opportunity to "fill us in" on various events which occurred before the opening of the novel but which are important to the plot. The information presented in this chapter also helps us to understand the motivation of characters such as Ganya and Nastasya

The chapter begins with a description of General Epanchin's wife and daughters. It seems that the General has been considering a marriage between his eldest daughter, Alexandra, and Totsky, but that his wife objects to the match and will not permit the matter to be mentioned to any of the girls.

Madame Epanchin's objections are based upon the relationship between Totsky and Nastasya. Totsky, who was Nastasya's guardian, apparently seduced her when she was sixteen. Four years later, it was rumored that Totsky planned to marry an heiress. Nastasya followed him to St. Petersburg, telling him that she forbade him to marry anyone, although she maintained that she herself did not care for him.

Nastasya remained in St. Petersburg, and Totsky, who was afraid of her, stayed a bachelor. At the time our story opens, Totsky, now wishing to marry Alexandra Epanchin, has decided to arrange a marriage for Nastasya. He and the General had told Nastasya of this and suggested Ganya as a suitable husband. Totsky offered Nastasya 75,000 roubles as a wedding present.

Much to their surprise, Nastasya indicated that she was very anxious to settle down and marry. However, she said she needed time to think about it because although she felt that Ganya loved her and would be a good husband, she did not know how his family would feel about their marriage.

Ganya's family did disapprove quite violently, and Nastasya heard about this, although she had not mentioned it to Ganya.

Comment: The Ivolgins, particularly Ganya's mother, felt that Nastasya as a "fallen woman" was not a suitable wife for Ganya. They belonged to that class of people who are "poor but genteel" and who, having known a higher position in society, wish to climb back to that position.

Nastasya also knew, by this time, that Ganya was mercenary, envious and vain, and that although he had originally found her attractive, he no longer loved her. Ganya intended to marry her for her money. He also planned to "revenge" himself on her after the wedding because he felt that marriage to her, although financially rewarding, would be socially degrading. Of course Nastasya did not know this.

Dostoyevsky also tells us that the General had a very personal interest in Ganya's courtship of Nastasya. The General was attracted to the girl and had bought an expensive pearl necklace to give her as a birthday present. News of this purchase had reached Madame Epanchin, as the General knew well, and he was afraid of the scolding she would give him. He was therefore very glad that the Prince had arrived, because this would take his wife's mind off her grievance.

PART I, CHAPTER 5

The General tells his wife and daughters, who are about to have lunch, about Prince Myshkin. He portrays the Prince as child-like, hungry and subject to fits. After questioning, he admits that Myshkin is really quite well-mannered, but is inclined to be "simple" at times. He then rushes off, stating that he is late for an appointment.

> Comment: We know that the General's "appointment" is merely a device for getting away from his wife's questions about the pearls. Madame Epanchin obviously knows this too.

During lunch, the Prince tells the Epanchins about himself and surprises them by behaving quite normally. After lunch, at the insistence of Madame Epanchin, Prince Myshkin describes his impressions of Switzerland: how at first he had been upset by its strangeness, but began to like the country after he saw an ass. This leads to some merry chatter on the part of the girls. Prince Myshkin defends the ass, stating that it is both useful and good-natured. Madame Epanchin declares herself to be good-natured to a fault and asks the Prince if he is good-natured.

> **Comment: The symbolism of the ass (or donkey), patient, hard-working and easily taken advantage of, is very interesting since these traits are later shown to be characteristics of Prince Myshkin. It should also be noted that Prince Myshkin is a Christ-figure, and an ass appears several times in Gospel stories about Christ.**

As the Prince tells the Epanchins about his thoughts in Switzerland, Adelaida, the second daughter, says that he seems to be a philosopher. Prince Myshkin agrees that perhaps he is, and that he may have come to teach. He goes on to say that even in prison one could find a great deal of life.

> **Comment: Here again we see Myshkin's relationship to Christ: he too is a philosopher and possibly a teacher. Since the Prince has previously declared that he knows little, he is obviously not planning to teach academic subjects.**

He then tells the Epanchins about a man he met who had been condemned to death but was reprieved at the last minute. Prince Myshkin describes the execution he had seen in France (the same one he told the footman about), and tells Adelaida that this would make a good subject for a painting. She however, responds to his directions concerning the picture by asking him to tell her whether he had ever been in love. Myshkin states that although he has never been in love, he has experienced happiness in a different way.

Comment: Myshkin's story of the condemned man's thoughts during what were supposedly his last five minutes is a description of Dostoyevsky's own experience in Semyonov Square.

PART I, CHAPTER 6

Prince Myshkin proceeds to tell the Epanchins the nature of the happiness he described in the previous chapter. During the four years he lived in Switzerland, he spent most of his time with the children of the village. He told them many things, concealing nothing from them, but most of the time he was just with them. He goes on to describe an unfortunate young woman of twenty, named Marie, who had been seduced and then abandoned. She had tuberculosis, but despite her illness had worked very hard to support her invalid mother. After her seduction, everyone in the village, including her mother, despised her. Marie's mother died two months later. No one would hire Marie or even give her anything to eat. The Prince felt very sorry for her, gave her some money, and kissed her.

Comment: The Prince explains to the Epanchins that he kissed Marie because he felt so sorry for her. Notice that after performing an act of Christian charity, Prince Myshkin gives Marie a kiss of Christian love.

Prince Myshkin says that the children, seeing him kiss Marie, told everyone about it. They then teased and chased Marie even more. After that the Prince began talking to them about her, telling them how unhappy she was. The children soon changed their attitude and came to love both Marie and the Prince. They thought he was in love with her and he did not contradict them. Finally, Marie died. The villagers were very angry with the Prince because of his influence over the children.

The Prince continues his recollections of his life in Switzerland, placing primary emphasis on his relations with the children. He says that Dr. Schneider (who was in charge of the clinic where the Prince stayed) thought he enjoyed being with the children because he was a child himself. However, Myshkin says that he preferred the children's company because he felt more comfortable with them than with adults.

Myshkin tells the Epanchins that although he was happy in Switzerland and did not want to leave, something occurred which made his return to Russia necessary.

Comment: The Prince is again referring to the "business matter he wanted to discuss with the General. We will learn later that this concerns an inheritance.

The chapter ends with the Prince telling the Epanchins what he sees in their faces. Alexandra seems kind-hearted, but the Prince also thinks that she has some secret trouble. Adelaida has a happy face and seems very understanding. Madame Epanchin strikes the Prince as being a child. He hastens to remind her how much he likes children, so that she will not be offended.

PART I, CHAPTER 7

After Myshkin finishes his tale, Madame Epanchin comments that she is indeed a child. Then she asks him why he did not analyze Aglaia, as he did the others. The Prince says that he is not ready to say anything about her yet, beyond admitting that she is almost as beautiful as Nastasya Filippovna. Madame Epanchin immediately asks where he saw Nastasya. When the Prince explains that he saw the portrait when Ganya showed it to the General, Madame Epanchin sends him to get it.

> **Comment: Aglaia has impressed the Prince as much as Nastasya has. He links the two of them together here, foreshadowing the relationship they will have to him and to each other.**

While the Prince is out of the room, the Epanchins discuss him. Adelaida thinks he is nice, but too simple. Alexandra agrees, but feels he is also somewhat ridiculous. Aglaia, on the other hand, feels Myshkin is less simple than he would have others think. Madame Epanchin defends him, saying that he is well aware of everything that goes on, but is also completely good. She sums up her opinion by saying that he is just like her.

> **Comment: Madame Epanchin's analysis of Prince Myshkin's character turns out to be correct. However, the feeling of the older girls that he is "too simple" has some truth in it also. As we will discover later, the Prince's naivete sometimes gets him into difficulties. Aglaia's criticism of him is without basis. The Prince surprises people by his intelligence because they expect him to be an "idiot".**

Myshkin finds Ganya still working in the General's study. Ganya criticizes him for mentioning the picture to the Epanchins and, in an undertone, calls him an "idiot." Then Ganya, who is obviously embarrassed, asks the Prince to do him a favor. He says that he has written a note to Aglaia, but is afraid to deliver it himself because the Epanchins are angry with him. He therefore asks the Prince to give the note to Aglaia, taking care that no one sees him do it. After some hesitation, the Prince agrees to be the messenger. He calms Ganya's unspoken fears by assuring him that he will not read the note. After the Prince leaves the study, Ganya demonstrates his anxiety over the note by pacing back and forth.

> **Comment: Ganya's rude behavior to the Prince show that he thinks the Prince really is an idiot. It also indicates that he is extremely worried. We learn the contents of the note later in this chapter.**

On his way back to the Epanchins, Myshkin stops to look at Nastasya's photograph again, hoping to confirm his initial impression of it. He feels that besides the great beauty of the face, it contains a mixture of contemptuous pride and child-like trust. The combination of these elements makes him feel sorry for her. The portrait shows a beauty which is almost painful to look at. Finally, Myshkin kisses the portrait.

> **Comment: It is obvious, from the amount of space which Dostoyevsky uses in describing and discussing Nastasya, that she will be an extremely important character in the novel. Although she has not yet made an appearance, we know quite a lot about her.**

The Prince gives Ganya's note to Aglaia. Then he shows the picture to the Epanchins. Only Adelaida admires it. The Prince explains that he admires Nastasya's beauty because her face shows great suffering. Suddenly, Madame Epanchin tells a servant to fetch Ganya. Alexandra seems dismayed at this, but Madame Epanchin says that she wants to talk to him. She adds that marriages are being arranged which are not to her liking.

Comment: Madame Epanchin is apparently referring to the match the General hopes to arrange between Alexandra and Totsky, as well as to that between Ganya and Nastasya.

When Ganya enters the room, Madame Epanchin immediately asks him if he is thinking about getting married. Ganya is very upset at this, and finally says that he is not. Madame Epanchin says that she will remember this. She gives the picture to Ganya, says she must go out, and takes leave of the Prince. She tells Myshkin that she hopes he will come to see her frequently, because she likes him and feels God sent him to St. Petersburg chiefly for her sake.

The girls leave and Ganya immediately turns on the Prince. He is very angry because he thinks the Prince told the Epanchins about his courtship of Nastasya. Myshkin assures him that he did not mention the matter, but Ganya refuses to believe him. Aglaia returns and asks Myshkin to write in her autograph album. Ganya pleads with her, saying that just a word from her will "save" him. She does not answer him, but tells the Prince to write that she does not make bargains. Then she asks Myshkin to come with her for a moment. As soon as they leave the room, she gives him Ganya's note and tells him to read it.

In his note, Ganya says that if Aglaia tells him to break his engagement to Nastasya, he will do so. He admits that he deserves nothing from her, but begs her to have pity on him. Aglaia explains to Myskin that Ganya really wants to marry her, but is afraid to refuse Nastasya and her money without an assurance that Aglaia will look favorably on his suit. Aglaia states that she might feel differently about Ganya if he were not so concerned about "playing it safe." She tells Myshkin to give the note back to Ganya and say that there is no answer. She also warns the Prince that Ganya will be very angry with him for returning the note.

Comment: Although Aglaia tells Myshkin that there is no answer to the note, she has already answered Ganya. When she told Myshkin to write that she did not make bargains, Ganya heard her. Ganya understands that this is her reply to his plea.

Ganya and the Prince leave the Epanchins' house to go to Ganya's. The Prince repeats what Aglaia told him. Ganya completely loses his self-control and rages against the Prince. He demands to know why the Prince has been confided in and what the Prince told the Epanchins. The Prince relates the subjects of his conversations with the Epanchins and assures Ganya that he did not tell them about Ganya's courtship of Nastasya. Finally, Ganya becomes so abusive that the Prince tells him he would prefer to stay at a hotel. Ganya apologizes and the Prince agrees to lodge with him.

Comment: The central event of this chapter is Ganya's note to Aglaia. Her rejection of Ganya's plea, Ganya's reaction, and the way in which she and Ganya act toward the Prince tell us a great deal about their characters; Aglaia is very independent and honest and expects others to be the same way. Ganya is quite childish, expecting to have things his way. He has temper tantrums when events do not turn out as he wishes.

PART I, CHAPTER 8

Ganya and the Prince arrive at the Ivolgin home. Ganya introduces the Prince to his mother, Nina Alexandrovna, and his sister, Varvara Ardalionovna, and then hurries out of the room with Ivan Petrovitch Ptitsyn, who has been visiting the women.

Comment: Ptitsyn is courting Varvara. Eventually they get married.

Kolya, Ganya's young brother, shows the Prince to his room. The Prince is soon visited by Ferdyshtchenko, the other lodger. He is a rather strange-looking person, with a unique manner. He cautions the Prince not to lend him any money.

As soon as he leaves, another odd person enters the room. He turns out to be Ganya's father, a retired general. He tells Myshkin that he knew his father well, and carried Myshkin around as a baby. General Ardalion Alexandrovitch Ivolgin also mentions the match between Ganya and Nastasya with great distaste. Nina Alexandrovna comes in and asks the Prince to come with her to the drawing room. Apparently, she wants to tell him something, but the General follows them and she becomes silent. General Ivolgin continues his conversation with the Prince, telling him facts about his parents which seem unbelievable. Finally, Varya (as Varvara Ivolgin is called) calls her father away.

As soon as he leaves, Nina Alexandrovna tells the Prince not to believe anything General Ivolgin says, and especially to avoid giving him any money.

Comment: General Ivolgin's stories attain fantastic heights at times. He apparently believes some of them himself, although he generally makes them up on the spur of the moment. The stories he tells Prince Myshkin about his parents are obviously extemporaneous.

Varya enters the drawing room and shows her mother the portrait of Nastasya Filippovna. They are quite upset, and plainly do not want Ganya to marry Nastasya. Ganya and Ptitsyn come in and Ganya, seeing the picture, accuses Myshkin of having told the family about it. Ptitsyn confesses that he is responsible, but Ganya does not apologize to the Prince. Ganya, Varya and their mother begin quarreling and the Prince leaves the room.

The Prince notices someone at the front door (the bell seems to be broken), opens it, and discovers Nastasya standing there. He recognizes her at once. She thinks he is a footman and becomes very angry because he does not take her coat at once. She tells him to announce her. Prince Myshkin announces Nastasya just as the Ivolgins are in the middle of their noisy fight.

Comment: Notice the expert way in which Dostoyevsky has built up the tensions surrounding Nastasya before introducing her. She has been mentioned in nearly every chapter thus far; we have been told of her early life; and her picture has caused controversy in both the Epanchin and the Ivolgin homes. Nothing could be more effective than her entrance here, announced by Prince Myshkin to a family which is quarreling over her.

PART I, CHAPTER 9

The Ivolgins are astounded at Nastasya's appearance. She has never before called on them, or even expressed a desire to meet them. She, however, seems to be in a good mood, and asks Ganya to introduce her. Varya is barely civil, but her mother makes appropriate welcoming remarks. Nastasya ignores Madame Ivolgin, asks Ganya where the lodgers are, and then begins laughing at him. Ganya is enraged, and when the Prince tries to calm him, turns on him menacingly. However, Ganya recovers his self-possession and introduces the Prince to Nastasya. Myshkin explains how he knew who she was. He is strangely moved, and Nastasya looks at him with great interest.

By now, everyone is in the drawing room. The last to make an appearance is General Ivolgin. He has dressed in evening clothes in honor of Nastasya. His family tries to get him to leave, because his presence is highly embarrassing. Ganya particularly is mortified. However, the old General stays and begins talking to Nastasya. He entertains her with a long story of an event which supposedly happened to him two years before. Finally, Nastasya comments that she read about the same incident in a newspaper a few days ago. Everyone is embarrassed, including the General, but he maintains that his story is true.

Ganya is very upset and tries once more to get his father to leave the room. At this moment, the doorbell rings violently.

Comment: As in the previous chapter, a moment of extreme tension is broken in a dramatic manner. We know that the new visitors will make as impressive an entrance as did Nastasya.

PART I, CHAPTER 10

A great many people, making considerable noise, enter the room. Myshkin recognizes Rogozhin and Lebedyev. They are accompanied by ten or twelve people, dressed in a variety of ways. Some of them seem drunk. Rogoshin sees Nastasya, concludes that she really is going to marry Ganya, and becomes furious with him. Ganya does not seem to recognize Rogozhin, so he identifies himself. He also says that he was cheated in a card game by Ganya. Then he says that Ganya will do anything for money. He announces that he has come to "buy" Ganya. Immediately after that, he asks Nastasya if she is going to marry Ganya. Nastasya acts surprised and says she has no intention of marrying him. Rogozhin throws a wad of notes (totaling 18,000 rubles) on the table without explaining why he does so. Nastasya, however, understands and laughs at him for trying to buy her favor with such a small sum. Rogozhin offers her forty thousand rubles, then a hundred thousand. He vows he will find the money by evening.

Comment: When we consider that Dostoyevsky was paid only some 5,000 rubles for *The Idiot*, these sums of money offered by Rogozhin attain greater significance.

By this time, everything is in an uproar. Varya demands that someone take Nastasya (whom she calls "shameless") away. Nastasya is insulted and tells Ganya that she only came to invite his mother and sister to her party. Ganya becomes even more upset and upbraids Varya. He is about to hit her when the Prince intervenes. As a result of his well-meant action, Myshkin is slapped by Ganya.

Comment: Among upper-class people, a slap in the face was so serious an insult that a duel followed almost invariably.

Instead of becoming angry, Prince Myshkin practically cries and tells Ganya that he will be very sorry for what he has done. Everyone crowds around the Prince, trying to comfort him.

Comment: Dostoyevsky's "crowd scenes" are superlatively done; they carry an atmosphere of confusion, almost frenzy, while making the action and relationships between the characters perfectly clear.

Rogozhin asks the Prince to come with him. Nastasya, serious now, looks at Myshkin searchingly. Myshkin tells Nastasya that she should be ashamed of herself, because she is not at all the way she seems now. Nastasya seems surprised, but before she leaves she kisses Madame Ivolgin's hand and says that the Prince is right. Ganya hurries after Nastasya. She asks him not to come with her now, but to be sure and come to her party in the evening. Ptitsyn leaves with Rogozhin and his friends, and as they go, Rogozhin tells Ganya that he has lost.

Comment: Prince Myshkin's statement that Nastasya is really quite different from the way she has acted will be repeated, more dramatically, at her birthday party.

By telling Ganya that he has lost, Rogozhin means that Ganya's complicated planning has had no result. Ganya will not marry either Aglaia or Nastasya, and he will never be rich.

PART I, CHAPTER 11

Kolya follows Myshkin to his room, hoping to be of some assistance. He tells the Prince that there will be an even more violent quarrel about Nastasya now. Myshkin sympathizes with Kolya over the family troubles, but Kolya says that it is their own fault. Kolya comments that Nastasya is very good looking. He is angry with Ganya because he is only marrying her for her money. Myshkin explains that he does not like Ganya, and Kolya says that this is perfectly understandable. They then talk about Varya, for whom Myshkin expresses admiration.

Varya comes into the room and tells Kolya to go away. She asks the Prince how he knew that Nastasya was acting strangely. She thinks his analysis is correct and comments that he seems to have considerable influence over Nastasya. As they are talking, Ganya enters to apologize to Myshkin.

Myshkin forgives Ganya and indicates surprise at the apology. He says he did not think Ganya would admit he was wrong. Ganya comments that the Prince is certainly no "idiot," but is very perceptive. Myshkin suggests that Ganya apologize to Varya, but he refuses.

Before leaving the room, Varya tells her brother that he would be miserable if he married Nastasya. Ganya asks the Prince for his opinion, and Myshkin states that the money would not be worth it. However, Ganya says that he has made up his mind to marry Nastasya. Myshkin expresses surprise at his assurance that Nastasya will accept him. Ganya says that Nastasya was not serious about Rogozhin's offer. Ganya maintains that Nastasya will marry him even though she despises him. He characterizes her as vain and foolish.

Comment: Ganya misjudges Nastasya and attributes to her his own personality traits.

Ganya goes on to say that he thinks Nastasya both loves and hates him. He also congratulates himself for the roughness with which he treated his sister, because he feels this shows to Nastasya that he is willing to abandon his family for her sake.

Then Ganya reflects that he is being extremely frank with the Prince. He explains this by saying that the Prince is one of the few really honest men he has ever met. He confesses that he is a scoundrel, and that for some reason, scoundrels are attracted to honest people. Finally, he says that he has been called a scoundrel by so many people that he has come to believe it himself. The Prince comforts him by saying he no longer thinks that Ganya is bad, but only a very ordinary, weak-willed character.

Comment: The Prince has analyzed Ganya correctly. However, as we shall see, Ganya would prefer being wicked to being the way he really is. Ganya is one of those unfortunate people who are so inadequate that they cannot even carry out evil intentions.

Ganya explains to the Prince that his chief object in wanting to marry Nastasya is not the money involved. He says that his ambition is to become rich so that he can be an "original" man.

Comment: Ganya apparently means that if he were rich, people would think him witty, wise and talented.

Ganya remarks that the Prince seemed quite impressed by Nastasya and asks if he loves her. Myshkin blushes, but says he is not in love. Then Ganya tells him that Nastasya is really virtuous.

After Ganya leaves, Kolya comes in and gives Myshkin a note from General Ivolgin. Kolya asks Myshkin not to tell the family about this. He also suggests that the Prince give the old man a little money. Myshkin states that he will be happy to see the General because he wants to ask him something.

Comment: In this chapter, we learn that Ganya wants to marry Nastasya so that he can use her money to become famous and popular in order to change his personality. His reasons just confirm our impression that Ganya is very foolish, vain and weak. No amount of money can change a person.

PART I, CHAPTER 12

Prince Myshkin goes to see General Ivolgin, who is drinking in a cafe. The General asks Myshkin for money, which the Prince readily agrees to lend him, although he has very little himself. Then Prince Myshkin asks the General to take him to Nastasya's party. General Ivolgin is very pleased, and pretends that it is his own idea. He announces that he will tell Ganya, at Nastasya's party, that if he marries her, the General will disown him.

The General goes on drinking and telling Myshkin stories, until the Prince insists that they go. By this time, the old man is very drunk, but in excellent spirits. On the way, he points out the homes of army friends. At one point, he insists on calling on one of them. Fortunately, since the General has mistaken the address, no one is home. Then the General insists that they call upon a dear friend of his, the widow Marfa Borissovna Terentyev. There they meet Kolya, who is a friend of the widow's eldest son, Ippolit. Kolya warns his father not to go into the house, because Marfa Borissovna expects him to repay the money she has lent him. However, the General insists on going in.

Comment: Marfa Borissovna is the General's mistress.

Madame Terentyev is very angry with the General. He gives her the twenty-five rubles which Myshkin had lent him. The Prince had only intended to give the General part of the money, for that was all he had. By this time, Prince Myshkin is convinced that the General will never take him to Nastasya's, so he asks Kolya to go with him.

On their way, Kolya tells Myshkin about Ippolit, who is his best friend. It seems that Ippolit is very ill with tuberculosis. He is also very upset about the General's affair with his mother. Kolya adds that he thinks it would be best for Ippolit to die soon. According to Kolya, his father gives Madame Terentyev money, which she lends back to him, with interest. Her family is in dire need, and Kolya's mother and sister help the children with food, money and clothes. Kolya says that Varya does this only because her mother does, but that his mother is genuinely sorry for the children. He adds that Ganya knows nothing of this. Kolya mentions that he and Ippolit would like to take an apartment together. Myshkin suggests that as soon as he has a job, all three of them should live together.

Myshkin explains to Kolya that Nastasya did not invite him to her party, but he wants to go anyway. He finds it difficult to explain why. They finally arrive at Nastasya's, and Kolya says goodbye to the Prince.

PART I, CHAPTER 13

Myshkin feels very unsure of himself as he enters Nastasya's home. He is mostly concerned with his object in coming. He wants to tell Nastasya that she should not marry Ganya, because he does not love her. He also has another object, which he cannot admit even to himself.

Comment: Although Myshkin has denied that he loves Nastasya, he obviously is very much in love with her.

Nastasya's apartment is rather small, but luxuriously furnished. Much to Myshkin's surprise, the maid shows no hesitation at seeing him (his dress is most unsuitable for an evening party) and goes to announce him at once. Gathered at Nastasya's is a small group of oddly assorted people. Among the guests are Totsky, General Epanchin, Ganya, Ptitsyn and Ferdyshtchenko. All of them are pre-occupied, and as a result there is no lively conversation. Ptitsyn, who has been with Rogozhin since the afternoon, announces that he will probably get the hundred thousand rubles he has promised Nastasya. Totsky and Ganya are concerned about what decision Nastasya will make. General Epanchin is quite upset, for his gift of pearls was accepted politely, but coldly. Ferdyshtchenko explains that he is there to "play the fool." He says that since he has no wit, he is permitted to be truthful.

Since the party is far from gay, all are glad to see Prince Myshkin. Nastasya apologizes for having forgotten to invite him. Myshkin whispers that she is perfect, but she tells him she is not. Nastasya offers her guests champagne, and drinks some herself. She looks and behaves so strangely that some of the guests suspect that she is feverish.

Ferdyshtchenko suggests that they play an odd parlor game in which each of the male guests relates his worst action. Nastasya urges that the game be played, and the men draw lots to see who will tell his story first.

PART I, CHAPTER 14

Ferdyshtchenko is the first to tell of his worst action. He repeats a story which he says he used on the other occasion he played this game. After a fairly long prologue, he relates the way in which he stole three rubles from a friend. The servant who was suspected was fired, but Ferdyshtchenko claims he still feels no remorse. Instead of applauding the story, as Ferdyshtchenko expects, Nastasya and her guests express contempt for him.

Ptitsyn refuses to join the game, but General Epanchin tells a tale of his youth. It seems that he had become angry with his former landlady for taking a bowl which belonged to him. He shouted and swore at her, but she made no response. Later that day, he found out that she was dying while he was yelling at her. He felt so sorry about this, that later he gave enough money to an old-people's home to support two old women. Ferdyshtchenko comments that instead of telling about his worst action, the General has narrated his best.

Totsky is the next to join in the game. His story describes the way in which he spoiled the chances of a friend who was in love. He did this by getting the only camellias left in the district for the lady after his friend told him he was going to buy them for her. Totsky states that he did this only from malice, not being attracted to the lady himself. As a result of his disappointment, the friend became very ill; when he recovered, he volunteered to fight in the Crimea, where he was soon killed.

Nastasya, whose mood seems to be getting progressively stranger, expresses boredom with the game and then suddenly tells Prince Myshkin that Totsky and the General want her to marry Ganya. She asks for the Prince's advice, saying that she will be guided by him. He tells her not to marry Ganya. Everyone is upset, and Totsky asks her why she should entrust such an important decision to Myshkin. She replies that he is the first person she has ever met whom she could trust as a true friend.

Ganya sarcastically thanks Nastasya for the considerate way in which she has refused him and implies that the Prince himself is after her money. Then Nastasya tells Totsky that she does not want his money or him either. She also tells the General to take back his pearls and give them to his wife. Then she announces that she will leave her apartment in the morning and begin a new life. Everyone is astonished. Just then, the doorbell rings. Nastasya seems relieved and Ptitsyn murmurs that this must be Rogozhin.

Comment: The violent ringing of the doorbell heralds a new and exciting development in the plot. Dostoyevsky indicates this by commenting that the bell rings just as it did in Ganya's flat. Although Nastasya's refusal of Ganya is dramatic, we can tell that the climax of the evening has not yet been reached.

PART I, CHAPTER 15

Nastasya's maid, Katya, comes in to say that a dozen drunken men (Rogozhin and his companions) are at the door. She is extremely alarmed, but Nastasya tells her not to worry and to show them in. The only one of Nastasya's guests who wishes to leave is General Epanchin; but when she tells him that he can go, he courteously states that he will remain to protect her. However, the General is concerned, primarily because of his social position, and whispers to Totsky that he thinks Nastasya has gone crazy. Totsky whispers back that she has always tended in that direction.

Rogozhin's party is much the same as that which so rudely descended on the Ivolgins. Rogozhin is now quite sober. He has spent the evening in getting together one hundred thousand rubles, much of it at a shocking interest rate. Rogozhin's followers are quite impressed at Nastasya's possessions and, when they see General Epanchin, most of them are overcome by shyness and return to the entrance hall. Lebedyev, however, is bolder than his companions and remains at Rogozhin's side.

Rogozhin looks at Nastasya with awe and silently puts a package on the table. When Nastasya asks him what is in the package, he says that it is the hundred thousand. She invites him and his companions to sit down, but most of them are too timid to join the party.

Nastasya explains to her guests how Rogozhin promised her this money. Then she asks Ganya if he really meant to marry her, a woman who would accept pearls from the General and money from Rogozhin. She also tells him that when she went to his home that afternoon, she wanted to see how far his folly would carry him. She did not expect him to be as low as he turned out to be. Then she adds that perhaps Rogozhin's earlier statement that Ganya would do anything for money, even crawl on all fours for it, is true. She cries that although she is shameless, Ganya is worse.

Comment: Ganya's reported willingness to do anything for money will play an exciting part in the next chapter.

The General pleads with her to return to her senses, but she says that she is a little drunk and is having a fling. Then she explains her relations with Totsky, saying that although she has not lived with him for five years, she has continued to let him support her. She concludes that the right place for her is in the streets. Finally, she says that either she will run away with Rogozhin, or go and become a washerwoman.

Nastasya repeats her declaration that she will leave her apartment in the morning, taking nothing with her. She declares that no one, not even Ferdyshtchenko, will want her when she is penniless. Ferdyshtchenko admits that he does not want her under those circumstances, but says that the prince does. Nastasya asks the Prince for confirmation, and he says that he will marry her. He adds that he does not think that she is a "fallen woman." Nastasya laughs and asks what they will live on. Prince Myshkin says that he loves her and will work, if necessary. He adds that he may be rich and pulls a letter out of his pocket. Ptitsyn offers to read the letter.

Comment: The letter which Myshkin produces concerns an inheritance. This is the "business" which he has referred to mysteriously several times, and which he wanted to discuss with General Epanchin earlier in the day. The Prince is so inexperienced in these matters that he is not sure that he has any claim to the inheritance.

PART I, CHAPTER 16

Ptitsyn reads Myshkin's letter and tells him that there is no reason to doubt its contents. According to the letter, which is from a highly reputable lawyer, Myshkin has inherited a fortune from an aunt he never knew. Everyone is astonished, for now the Prince is even richer than Rogozhin.

Nastasya acts even more strangely than she did before. First, she says, almost to herself, that now she is a Princess. Then she calls for champagne and tells everyone to congratulate her and the Prince. Rogozhin is terribly upset and urges her to marry him. Nastasya laughs at him and then asks Prince Myshkin if he will not be ashamed of having a wife with such a disreputable background.

Prince Myshkin assures Nastasya that he loves her and thinks that she is honoring him by accepting his proposal. She is amazed because no one has ever talked to her like this before. Nastasya next asks Rogozhin where he planned to take her, and at his reply, states that perhaps she will go with him after all. Jumping up, she says that she could not possibly marry the Prince because she would ruin him by doing so.

Nastasya tells the Prince that he should marry Aglaia Epanchin. Then she tells Ganya that he could have married Aglaia, if he had not tried to bargain with her. Commenting that men are all alike, she says that they should choose either virtuous women or immoral women, and not try to have both.

Comment: Nastasya has foreseen what will be a grave problem for Prince Myshkin. Later on, he will have to make a choice between her and Aglaia. He does make the choice, but the results are disastrous. In contrast, Ganya has been unable to choose between the two women. As a result, neither will accept him.

Rogozhin is practically delirious with joy. In answer to Nastasya's question, he confirms that the hundred thousand rubles are hers, to do with as she wishes. She tells Ganya that she is going to throw the money into the fire and if he will retrieve it with his bare hands, the money will be his. Everyone is greatly upset and urges her not to go through with this crazy plan, but she throws in the bundle. However, Ganya stands motionless. Lebedyev pleads that he be allowed to save the money, but she refuses to let him come near.

Finally, as the notes catch fire, Ganya faints. Nastasya removes the bundle from the fire. Fortunately, only the outside wrapper is burned. Nastasya tells everyone that Ganya is to have the money after all, because he has proved that his pride is stronger than his avarice. Then she leaves with Rogozhin. Prince Myshkin follows them.

Totsky and Ivan Ptitsyn sum up the situation by commenting that Nastasya has acted the part of a fallen woman primarily to spite Totsky. Totsky compares her to an uncut diamond, for she is beautiful and intelligent, but needs someone to guide and control her.

Comment: This chapter, which concludes the first part of *The Idiot*, is a climactic one. These are the chief events:

1) **Prince Myshkin, who seemed penniless is discovered to be wealthy.**

2) **Nastasya, who has refused Ganya, first accepts and then rejects Prince Myshkin.**

3) **Nastasya tells Ganya that he can have Rogozhin's hundred thousand rubles if he will pull it out of the fire. When he refuses, she gives it to him anyway.**

4) **Nastasya finally decides to go off with Rogozhin. The Prince follows them.**

THE IDIOT

PART II

PART II, CHAPTER 1

Comment: This chapter serves as an interlude. It marks the passage of time between the first and second parts of *The Idiot* and summarizes briefly the events occurring in the six- month interval which separates the first and second parts.

Prince Myshkin leaves St. Petersburg for Moscow two days after the events described in Part I. Officially he leaves to claim his inheritance, but Dostoyevsky hints that Myshkin's hasty departure may have something to do with Nastasya. Little is known of his activities during the six months of the Prince's absence from St. Petersburg.

About a month after his departure, Madame Epanchin receives a letter from her old friend and social superior, Princess Byelokonsky. The Princess writes from Moskow that Prince Myshkin has called on her and made so favorable an impression that she has invited him to visit her daily. Madame Epanchin is quite pleased at this news and reverts to her original favorable impression of the Prince. General Epanchin tells his family that he has learned that the Prince's fortune is not as large as it was first thought to be. There are debts and other claims on it. On top of all this, Prince Myshkin proves himself totally lacking in business sense. He pays all creditors whether they have proof of their claim or not.

Nastasya Filippovna deserted Rogozhin the day after her famous party. Rogozhin found her in Moscow and she finally agreed to marry him. However, just before the wedding, she disappeared again. Prince Myshkin also vanished at the same time.

Dostoyevsky also tells us about the other principal characters in the story. Ganya Ivolgin begged the Prince to return Nastasya's hundred thousand rubles to her and then fell ill. After his recovery, he resigned from his job. We are told that he never goes anywhere, but sits at home, brooding. Varya Ivolgin married Ptitsyn, partly, according to the rumors, because Ganya was incapable of supporting his family. Ferdyshtchenko left the Ivolgins soon after Prince Myshkin did. No one knows where he is, but it is rumored that he is drinking. The entire Ivolgin family has moved in with Ptitsyn and Varya. General Ivolgin, however, has been put in debtors' prison because he cannot pay what he owes Madame Terentyev. Varya has become friendly with the Epanchin girls and Kolya is a great favorite with Madame Epanchin.

Totsky never proposed to Alexandra and has married a French-woman. Adelaida is engaged to Prince S. A friend of his, Yevgeny Pavlovitch Radomsky, an Imperial aide-de-camp, is quite interested in Aglaia. Because of this, the Epanchins' plans to go abroad have been put off.

Comment: Dostoyevsky never mentions Prince S.'s full
name. However, David Magarshack, in his introduction
to his translation of *The Idiot*, indicates that the last
name was originally Shcherbakov.

About Easter time, Kolya Ivolgin receives a short note from the
Prince, asking him to give a sealed letter to Aglaia Epanchin. In
his letter the Prince says nothing about himself, but declares that
he thinks of Aglaia often, wants her to remember him, and wants
her to be happy. Aglaia is troubled about this communication
and decides not to show it to anyone. She puts it away in a book.
When she notices, a few days later, that the title of the book is
Don Quixote de la Mancha, she laughs.

Comment: Dostoyevsky does not tell us why Aglaia
laughs at finding she had put Myshkin's letter in *Don
Quixote*. However, we will find out later in the novel
that Aglaia associates the Prince with *Don Quixote*. *Don
Quixote*, the hero of Cervantes' novel, called himself
"the knight of the sad countenance." Prince Myshkin
bears some resemblance to this character for, as
pointed out in the Introduction, they are both fighting
for lost causes. *Don Quixote* fights against imaginary
enemies, for example, windmills, using the outmoded
methods of knightly combat. Prince Myshkin, on the
other hand, is trying to use the Christian virtues to
combat the evil in the world. As Dostoyevsky shows,
his struggle is useless; both his methods and his aim
are futile in the modern world.

Comment (Additional): In this introductory chapter,
we learn the following facts:

1) Prince Myshkin and Rogozhin are still pursuing Nastasya.

2) Ganya gave back the hundred thousand rubles and, after a serious illness, became a recluse.

3) Varvara Ivolgin is married to Ptitsyn.

4) General Ivolgin has been put in jail for failing to pay his debts.

5) Totsky did not propose to Alexandra and has married a Frenchwoman.

6) Adelaida is engaged to Prince S.

7) Prince Myshkin cares quite a lot about Aglaia.

PART II, CHAPTER 2

It is June. Prince Myshkin arrives in St. Petersburg from Moscow. No one knows he is coming, but as he leaves the train station, he is aware that someone is looking at him intently. He goes straight to Lebedyev's house. The family is in mourning, for Lebedyev's wife died five weeks ago. There are four children, the eldest of whom, Vera, holds the baby. Lebedyev's nephew is also present. Lebedyev is already somewhat drunk, and his daughter explains that he will become worse as the day goes on.

Apparently, Lebedyev has written to the Prince about Nastasya Filippovna. It seems that she ran away from Rogozhin again and came to Lebedyev. Lebedyev says that she asked him to protect her, particularly from the Prince. However, it appears that he has brought her together with Rogozhin again. She is living with Lebedyev's sister-in-law, but Lebedyev notes that she may have gone to Pavlovsk by this time, to stay with her friend Darya Alexeyevna. Lebedyev reports that Nastasya is not looking forward to her marriage to Rogozhin and is in a bad humor. He states that he has tried to "comfort" her by interpreting the Apocalypse, which seems to be one of his hobbies, but that only makes her more angry.

Comment: The Apocalypse is the last book of the New Testament, which is also known as Revelations, or the Revelations of St. John the Divine. It is a prophetic book, concerned with the end of the world, the Last Judgment and the coming of Anti-Christ. The prophecies are extremely ambiguous and there has been considerable controversy concerning the meaning of the book; new interpretations arise frequently.

When Prince Myshkin asks Lebedyev his name and patronymic, Lebedyev first says it is Timofey Lukyanovitch. His nephew laughs at him and says he cannot tell the truth even about his name, which is Lukyan Timofeyevitch.

Comment: This is the first time we are told Lebedyev's full name. Besides the first name, all Russians have a middle name (or patronymic) which indicates the first name of their father. The "vitch" means "son of," whereas "vna" indicates "daughter of."

Lebedyev's nephew says that his uncle is always trying to cheat people, and accuses him of defending a dishonest money lender simply because of the fee. Lebedyev counters by saying that his nephew is a rebel, a plotter, and a future murderer. The nephew then says that his uncle is so depraved that he recently prayed for the repose of Madame Du Barry's soul. Lebedyev explains who Madame Du Barry was, and defends himself by saying that he only prayed for her and other great sinners.

Comment: Madame Du Barry was the mistress of Louis XV of France. She was guillotined during the French Revolution.

Lebedyev tells the Prince that the Epanchins are at Pavlovsk, a summer resort, and that Kolya is either with them or with his father, at a hotel.

Comment: The Prince has paid General Ivolgin's debts.

He says that he himself is taking his family to Pavlovsk in a few days. The Prince finds out that Lebedyev is going to occupy a small cottage belonging to Ptitsyn, but that the main house is unoccupied. The Prince indicates a desire to rent the villa. As Myshkin leaves, Lebedyev notices that he is more than usually preoccupied.

PART II, CHAPTER 3

After leaving Lebedyev's, the Prince wanders through St. Petersburg looking for a particular house. He finally finds the house, which is large and gloomy; it is Rogozhin's. Rogozhin opens the door, looking very startled to see Myshkin. Myshkin asks if he knew he was coming to St. Petersburg that day, and explains that he felt someone in the crowd at the station was watching him in just the way that Rogozhin looked at him. Rogozhin is suspicious but does not reply. He obviously does not like the Prince.

Myshkin asks Rogozhin about his family, and then about Nastasya. He says that he has never tried to interfere in their relationship, and will not do so now. However, he adds that he thinks she is both physically and mentally ill. He repeats his previous contention that a marriage between Nastasya and Rogozhin would ruin them both. Then, after explaining once more that he pities Nastasya rather than loves her, Prince Myshkin gets up to go.

Rogozhin, however, asks him to stay, and says he is becoming fond of him again. He begins to tell the Prince of his troubles with Nastasya. She hates him, he realizes, and does things just to annoy him. He also states that he is afraid to go and see her. Myshkin asks why Rogozhin is intent on marrying her, if he knows all this. Rogozhin does not answer. Then Rogozhin says that at one time, in Moscow, he became so angry with her that he beat her. Afterward, he begged her forgiveness for thirty-six hours. She laughed at him and told him the story about the emperor who stood barefoot in the snow for three days, begging forgiveness from the Pope, while vowing revenge in his heart. Rogozhin admitted that he might be doing the same thing. Finally, she forgave him and agreed to set a wedding date, but ran off to St. Petersburg a week later.

Comment: The story Nastasya tells Rogozhin about the emperor and the Pope refers to Emperor Henry IV of Germany and Pope Gregory VII. They quarrelled over Henry's claim of jurisdiction over the German bishops. Finally Gregory excommunicated Henry. In 1075, Henry went to Canossa, in Italy, to beg the Pope to forgive him. After watching him stand barefoot in the snow for three days, Gregory did forgive him. Henry was very angry, and a few years later, set up a rival pope.

Rogozhin says that it appears the Prince's pity is stronger than his own love for Nastasya. Myshkin comments that Rogozhin's love and hate for her are practically identical. He starts to say something else, but Rogozhin interrupts, asking Myshkin if he thinks he (Rogozhin) will murder Nastasya. Myshkin says that this is possible, and wonders why Nastasya has anything at all to do with Rogozhin.

Then Myshkin notices a picture of Rogozhin's father and comments that if Rogozhin had not developed such a passionate love for Nastasya, he probably would have become just like his father. Rogozhin's father's one consuming interest was in making, and keeping, money. Rogozhin agrees and says that Nastasya said the same thing. She analyzed him as being a man of strong passions and also complimented him on his intelligence, despite his lack of education.

Comment: Myshkin and Nastasya are right about Rogozhin. He is a very passionate character, so much so that he is capable of murder, as we shall see. He is also quite insecure. He realizes that he is uneducated and feels very uncomfortable in "society." He thinks less well of himself than others think of him, and takes pride in Nastasya's statement that he is intelligent. Obviously, he always thought of himself as being rather stupid.

Prince Myshkin tells Rogozhin that Nastasya must have faith in his good qualities, or she would never consider marrying him. He says that Nastasya would be going to her death knowingly otherwise. Rogozhin looks at Prince Myshkin in amazement and states that Nastasya is marrying him because she expects to be murdered. He also states that she loves Myshkin, but does not think she can marry him because she would disgrace him. Rogozhin declares that Nastasya would have committed suicide long ago, if she thought Rogozhin would not kill her. He sums up his analysis by saying that when Nastasya marries him, it will be out of spite.

While Rogozhin is speaking, Myshkin is looking at a knife he has found on the table. Rogozhin snatches it out of his hand. However, as Myshkin says goodbye, he forgetfully picks up the knife again. Rogozhin takes it away from him. Myshkin asks him about the knife, and Rogozhin says that it is a garden knife, but that he uses it to cut book pages.

Comment: This chapter prepares us for much that will occur later in the novel. Myshkin and Rogozhin, in speaking of Nastasya, bring up the subject of murder. In Part I, Myshkin hinted that he was afraid Rogozhin might murder Nastasya; he repeats his fear now, in stronger language. Oddly enough, Rogozhin does not deny this possibility, and even states that Nastasya will marry him as a form of suicide.

The chapter ends with Myshkin seeing and commenting on Rogozhin's knife. Rogozhin becomes much more upset over the knife than seems normal. The knife has obviously been purchased recently, and Rogozhin seems to intend to use it for something other than cutting pages. Since the knife enters the conservation just after Myshkin and Rogozhin are speaking of murder, we can easily guess that Rogozhin plans to murder Nastasya with the knife.

PART II, CHAPTER 4

Rogozhin shows Myshkin out of the house. They pass through several rooms in which there are paintings. Myshkin is struck by one, which he says seems to be a very good copy of a Holbein he saw in Switzerland.

> **Comment: Dostoyevsky does not describe this picture now, but later on in *The Idiot* (Part III, Chapter 6), Ippolit will talk about it at greater length. The picture, by Hans Holbein (1497?–1543) shows Christ taken from the Cross. The artist's interpretation is unusual, because he shows Christ looking very dead indeed and bearing the marks of terrible suffering. Dostoyevsky was greatly impressed when he saw this painting in Basel in 1867.**

Rogozhin asks Myshkin if he believes in God. Before answering the question, Myshkin comments that the Holbein picture could cause one to lose his faith. Rogozhin replies that it is doing just that. Then Myshkin tells Rogozhin about some people he met the previous week. One was an extremely well-educated man who was an atheist. The same evening, Myshkin stopped at a hotel where everyone was discussing a recent murder. A peasant killed his friend to get his watch, and prayed to God for forgiveness while he was committing the murder. The following morning, Myshkin relates, a drunken soldier sold him a "silver" cross (obviously made of tin) and looked quite pleased with himself at having successfully cheated the Prince. The final **episode** which the Prince describes concerns a peasant woman who, when her infant smiled for the first time, crossed herself. She explained that just as she was glad when the child smiled, God was glad every time a sinner prayed.

After telling of these incidents, Myshkin says that the essence of religious feeling has nothing to do with rational thought and is not affected by crime. He affirms that this religious feeling is more evident in Russia than anywhere else. Then he says that there is much work to be done in Russia.

> **Comment: Although Myshkin does not actually answer Rogozhin's question, it is obvious that he does believe in God. The point of his stories is that religious feeling cannot be measured by external signs. Even the atheist, while denying God with his lips, has a religious instinct in his heart. The Prince seems to be saying that the Russian people have a greater capacity for religious passion than anyone else, but that they do not necessarily believe in God. Myshkin's declaration that there is much work to be done in Russia refers to his "mission": he hopes to rekindle the flame of Christian love. When the Russian people once more practice the Christian virtues, particularly love (Christ's commandments in Matthew 22:36–40 are to love God and to love one's neighbor as one's self), they will be able to convert the rest of the world. Dostoyevsky believed in the "sacred mission" of the Russian people. However, he was more concerned with Christianity as a way of life than with the externals of organized religion.**

As Myshkin leaves, Rogozhin suddenly asks him if he has the tin cross he bought from the soldier. He requests Myshkin to exchange that cross for his one gold one. The Prince, after initial hesitation, is pleased and comments that now they will be brothers. Then Rogozhin takes Myshkin to see his mother, who is old and senile. He tells her what has happened and asks her to bless Myshkin, which she readily does. As they part, Myshkin tries to embrace Rogozhin. At first, he refuses. Then, he laughingly says he will not murder Myshkin for his watch, embraces him and tells him to take Nastasya.

Comment: This is an extremely important and difficult chapter. Dostoyevsky continues his development of Myshkin as a Christ-figure, and of Rogozhin as his opposite. Myshkin, being human (in other words, having Rogozhin's evil qualities within himself although they cannot be translated into action), is able to understand Rogozhin's feelings and to realize the extent to which Rogozhin's passion may carry him. Rogozhin, on the other hand, has considerable insight into his own emotions and is afraid of them. When Myshkin describes the peasant who asked forgiveness while cutting his friend's throat, Rogozhin laughs because he recognizes the absurdity of this act (the peasant was sincerely penitent while committing his crime) and, more important, because he knows himself capable of just such an act.

Myshkin had to buy the tin cross from the soldier because he, as a Christ-figure, must carry the burden of the sins of those who, like the soldier, would sell their God; he must bear the Cross. Rogozhin wants that particular tin cross because he feels that wearing it (that is, taking up Myshkin's burden) will prevent him from killing Nastasya.

PART II, CHAPTER 5

Myshkin calls on General Epanchin, but he is not home. Then he goes to the hotel where Kolya has been staying. Kolya is not there, but he has left a message that if he is not back by mid-afternoon, it will mean that he has gone to Pavlovsk with Madame Epanchin. The Prince waits for him for a while, and then wanders around the city. He finds himself near the railway station, buys a ticket to Pavlovsk, but suddenly throws the ticket away and leaves the station. He feels very confused and finally realizes that he has been looking for something for several hours. Then he remembers that when he discovered that he was looking for something, he was standing in front of a shop window. He feels that he must find the shop, to ascertain whether he is dreaming or not. The Prince does not feel well and, in fact, his sensations are very similar to those which used to precede an epileptic attack.

The Prince notes that he was looking at a particular item in the shop window, which cost sixty kopeks, but he cannot remember what it was. He finds the shop about a block away and sees the sixty kopek article. Then he recalls that the first time he stood in front of the shop, he felt Rogozhin's eyes looking at him, just as they had been at the train station that morning.

The Prince begins thinking about his feelings just before an epileptic attack. At these times he is sad and depressed, but suddenly he becomes calm and joyful. All of his perceptions are heightened, particularly his sense of being. He feels at these moments that he understands everything, even the paradoxical statement that time shall be no more. Prince Myshkin feels that this moment of complete insight is so wonderful that it is worth having the disease.

Comment: Dostoyevsky is here explaining his own experiences. In a letter to a friend, he wrote that he felt so happy in the few seconds preceding the actual onset of an epileptic fit, that he would gladly shorten his life by ten years for those few seconds of joy.

Prince Myshkin sits down and alternately thinks about his happiness just before a fit and his present feeling of despair and foreboding. Suddenly, he gets up and begins to look for the house Nastasya is staying at. He says to himself that she has probably gone to Pavlovsk, but for some reason he feels compelled to go to the house. On the way, he keeps thinking about Lebedyev's family, particularly his nephew. Lebedyev had introduced his nephew as a future murderer, and Myshkin mentally confuses him with a murderer all St. Petersburg is talking about. This leads Myshkin to think about Rogozhin and the possibility that he may use his "garden" knife to kill Nastasya. Then Myshkin criticizes himself severely for assuming Rogozhin to be capable of such a crime. From a feeling of intense despair, Myshkin's mood suddenly changes to one of joy. He is certain that his illness (epilepsy) is returning, but he feels quite happy. He is most anxious to see Nastasya and now feels nothing but love toward Rogozhin. He continues to muse and then, without warning, he painfully recalls his distress when he realized that Nastasya was going mad. He knows too that Rogozhin's suspicions of Nastasya are a symptom of insanity.

Myshkin feels that Rogozhin is capable of pity and already shows signs of it. To the Prince, pity or compassion is the most important emotion. He reflects that Rogozhin is in need of compassion, for he is losing his faith. Myshkin realizes that Rogozhin must be suffering and has a great desire to be able to believe in something or someone.

Comment: Prince Myshkin, of course, is capable of infinite compassion for all men. Whether he realizes it himself or not, he is the someone in whom Rogozhin wants to believe. Thus, Rogozhin's act of wanting to exchange crosses with the Prince takes on greater significance. This episode makes them "brothers," as the Prince points out. Rogozhin seems to feel that he can obtain Myshkin's love and pity only if they are

"brothers." However, no external force is needed to tie them together.

Myshkin finally arrives at the house where Nastasya has been staying. He is told that she has gone to Pavlovsk for a few days. As he leaves, he is aware that his purpose in going to the house was to see Rogozhin's eyes once more. Myshkin wonders why he does not go up to Rogozhin. By this time he has returned to his hotel. His thoughts are confused and he is filled with foreboding, but he does not admit to himself what he is afraid of. He remembers Rogozhin's knife, and then recalls the article in the shop window. He wonders what connection there is between the two objects and then realizes what the link between them is.

Comment: Dostoyevsky does not tell us what the sixty-kopek item is, but we can deduce that it is a knife. Myshkin's sudden realization of the connection between the two knives is shocking to him because it forces him to be aware of his identity with Rogozhin. Myshkin and Rogozhin are, in a way, one character, with Myshkin having almost divine goodness, and Rogozhin embodying diabolical evil. Therefore, Myshkin is fascinated by the knife in the shop window as he was with Rogozhin's knife because he has, on an unconscious level, the same passions that Rogozhin has on a conscious level. Of course, Myshkin is incapable of using a knife, even in self-defense, because his is essentially a passive nature.

As Myshkin reaches his hotel, a thunderstorm breaks. Several people run into the hotel for shelter, and he knows that Rogozhin is one of them. He quickly follows him up a dark stairway and finds him hidden in a turning of the staircase. Rogozhin raises his hand, in which he holds a knife, but the Prince does not even try to ward off the blow. Later, Myshkin thought that he cried out his disbelief in Rogozhin's act at this point. Then, Myshkin has a moment of intense self-knowledge, screams, and has an epileptic attack. He falls down the stairs and Rogozhin runs away. Kolya turns up at this point, helps Myshkin, and takes him to Lebedyev's. Three days later, they all go to Pavlovsk.

Comment: This chapter, which reveals the inner thoughts of Prince Myshkin, leads up to a surprising climax. Earlier in the chapter, Myshkin feels that he is going to have an epileptic fit. This accounts for his strange mood-swings, from despair to joy and back again. However, his presentiment does not involve only the epileptic attack. The emphasis on knives leads us to believe that Myshkin foresees that Rogozhin will try to kill him. He is saved by his fit, for Rogozhin becomes frightened and runs away without stabbing him. Myshkin has no real fear of death and, in fact, would probably prefer to sacrifice himself. However, he obviously still has work to do.

PART II, CHAPTER 6

Three days after Myshkin's epileptic attack, he goes to Pavlovsk with Kolya, Lebedyev and his family. General Ivolgin is one of the party. Lebedyev is so anxious to make the Prince comfortable that he annoys him by keeping people away from him and poking his head in the door at frequent intervals to see if everything is all right. Prince Myshkin mentions this and Lebedyev is immediately very apologetic. However, he does not change his ways.

Kolya comes in to announce that Madame Epanchin and her daughters are coming to visit the Prince. They have just learned of the Prince's illness. Madame Epanchin is so sure that he is dying that she is almost disappointed to see him looking so well. Madame Epanchin very quickly loses all patience with Lebedyev, who behaves in his usual silly manner. She also becomes annoyed with General Ivolgin and tells him to go and repent of his sins. However, when he takes her at her word, she feels sorry for him.

Suddenly, Kolya brings up the subject of the "poor knight." Everyone laughs except Aglaia, who is angry, and the Prince, who is embarrassed. Kolya says that a month before, Aglaia, when looking through *Don Quixote*, declared that there was nothing better than the "poor knight."

Comment: Aglaia had put Prince Myshkin's letter to her (Part II, Chapter 1) in *Don Quixote*.

Prince S. explains to Madame Epanchin that there is a fragmentary Russian poem by Alexander Pushkin called "The Poor Knight," and that Aglaia suggested that Adelaida use it as the subject for her next painting. Madame Epanchin declares that all this is very foolish, but Aglaia says that nothing but respect is meant. She says that the poem describes a man with an ideal which he pursues against all odds. Aglaia goes on to say that "The Poor Knight" is just like Don Quixote except that he is serious rather than comical.

At the request of her mother, Aglaia gets up to recite the poem. She faces Prince Myshkin, who is extremely embarrassed. Just as she is about to begin, General Epanchin enters with a young man.

Comment: Prince Myshkin's reaction to this discussion reveals that he knows Aglaia identifies him with the "poor knight." Aglaia's statement that she respects the "poor knight" shows her feelings about the Prince. The identification of Myshkin as the "poor knight" will be even clearer in the next chapter.

PART II, CHAPTER 7

General Epanchin enters, accompanied by Yevgeny Pavlovitch Radomsky. At the time, Aglaia is reciting Pushkin's poem, so no introductions are made. Prince Myshkin, however, recognizes the young man as Radomsky, although he has never met him. Aglaia recites the poem with sincere simplicity.

"The Poor Knight" describes a crusader with a vision to which he remains loyal. The only identifying mark on his person is the monogram "A.M.D." on his shield. Finally he dies, insane. When reciting the poem, Aglaia inserts the letters "N.F.B." in place of "A.M.D."

Comment: The initials N.F.B. are those of Nastasya Filippovna Barashkov.

Madame Epanchin is unfamiliar with the poem, but seems to realize that Aglaia is referring to Prince Myshkin. She whispers to Aglaia that she has recited well, but that her purpose is unkind. Then Madame Epanchin expresses great interest in Pushkin and insists that she must read some of his works at once. Lebedyev offers her his own set, for the price which he paid.

Following the recitation, conversation becomes general again. Myshkin and Radomsky are introduced. Radomsky has perplexed every one by appearing in civilian dress. He explains that he has wanted to resign his army commission for some time, and finally has done so. However, he adds that he intends to return to the army after about a year.

Vera Lebedyev tells the company that four men are waiting outside, but her father will not allow them to enter. Lebedyev says that one of them is the "son of Pavlishtchev" and that Ganya and Ptitsyn have been trying to talk to them. The Prince is distressed and comments that he thought Ganya was taking care of them.

Just then, Ganya and Ptitsyn come in. Madame Epanchin seems to know what is going on, and suggests that the men be invited in so that the Prince can settle the business once and for all. In answer to a question, Lebedyev says that the men are not nihilists, but have gone further than nihilism, in that they act rather than just talk. Lebedyev says that these men believe that if they want anything, they should take it even if they have to kill people. Myshkin tells Lebedyev that he is wrong, and that these men are just misguided. The Prince apologizes to his guests for this interruption. As he ushers the men in, he suspects that someone has arranged that they come at this moment to humiliate him in front of the Epanchins. Then, however, he feels ashamed of his skeptical thoughts.

Three of the visitors are very young. They introduce themselves as Antip Burdovsky (who also calls himself "Pavlishtchev's son"), Vladimir Doktorenko (Lebedyev's nephew) and Ippolit Terentyev. The fourth member of the group, who is somewhat older, gives his name simply as Keller. Myshkin recognizes him as "the boxer" in Rogozhin's band of followers. At first they are silent, looking as though waiting for someone to begin.

Comment: We will see what business the young men have with Prince Myshkin in the following chapter. Pavlishtchev, you will recall, was Prince Myshkin's benefactor during his youth. It was he who paid for the Prince's stay in the Swiss sanitorium.

PART II, CHAPTER 8

Prince Myshkin begins by telling the young men that he would prefer to discuss their business in another room. Burdovsky and Ippolit complain of his treatment of them, for making them wait in the hall for two hours. The Prince asserts that he has just learned of their arrival and again entreats them to go with him to another room.

Madame Epanchin interrupts, telling Myshkin to read a newspaper article, which Lebedyev has brought to her attention. The Prince expresses unwillingness to read it aloud and she orders Kolya to do it. The article, without mentioning any names, of course, tells Myshkin's history in a libelous fashion. The point of the story is that the "idiot," who has inherited a fortune, refuses to give any of the money that his benefactor, "P.", squandered on his education, to "P.'s" illegitimate son. The article ends with some satirical verses contributed by an unidentified person.

The Prince is horribly embarrassed and deeply hurt by this malicious article. The Epanchins are also uncomfortable. Ippolit and Burdovsky seem surprised, Doktorenko is displeased, but Keller seems rather proud. Myshkin denies that there is any truth in the article and declares he would be greatly surprised if any of the four young men had written it. Ippolit immediately states that he knows nothing about it, and does not approve of it.

Doktorenko confesses that he knew about the article, but would have advised against its publication. Something in Burdovsky's manner makes the Prince ask if he is responsible for the article. Myshkin adds that it seems contradictory for Burdovsky to publicize his claim and yet resent having the Prince talk about it in front of his friends.

Doktorenko loudly acknowledges that Burdovsky has no legal claim, but maintains that morally he is in the right. He adds that Burdovsky does not entreat the Prince for money, but demands it, as a right. He says that Keller wrote the article, without the approval of the rest of them. Keller admits authorship of the article, but says that someone else wrote the poem.

Myshkin states his opinion that Burdovsky's lawyer initiated the scheme, taking advantage of Burdovsky's naivete. He recalls that at first the whole story sounded made-up, and he could not believe that Burdovsky would permit his mother to be so dishonored. However, based on his feeling that Burdovsky had been victimized, the Prince says that he planned to give him ten thousand rubles. Myshkin states that this is all Pavlishtchev could have spent on him. Burdovsky, Ippolit and Doktorenko shout that this is too little, but Keller advises them to take the money.

The Prince goes on to say that Ganya has obtained proof that Burdovsky is not Pavlishtchev's son at all. However, Myshkin continues to emphasize his belief that Burdovsky has been misled. He also implies that Burdovsky is simple like himself. Then the Prince states that he will give Burdovsky the ten thousand rubles he planned to use for founding a school in Pavlishtchev's memory. Prince Myshkin asks Ganya to explain the details concerning his "detective" work and sits down. The Prince already regrets his choice of words in speaking to Burdovsky and calls himself a real "idiot."

Comment: Here again, Myshkin shows himself painfully honest. He says exactly what he thinks, but quickly realizes how tactless his remarks are.

PART II, CHAPTER 9

Ganya begins his recital of the facts he has learned by stating that Burdovsky was born two years after his parents' marriage. In addition, he states that letters have proved that Pavlishtchev went abroad one and a half years before Burdovsky's birth and remained out of the country for three years. Ganya explains that Pavlishtchev took great interest in Burdovsky's mother because he had been fond of her sister, and supported her until his death. Ganya says that Pavlishtchev's relatives got the idea that Burdovsky was Pavlishtchev's son, but that his mother emphatically denied it. When asked why he is going into such detail, Ganya states that the facts prove that Burdovsky did not intend to deceive anyone, but really believed himself to be Pavlishtchev's son.

Burdovsky gets up to leave, declaring that he will not accept Prince Myshkin's charity, and gives him back an envelope which he says contains two hundred and fifty rubles. Actually, as Ganya discovers, there are only one hundred rubles in the envelope. Doktorenko explains that the hundred and fifty missing rubles were used to pay the lawyer, but will be returned to the Prince as soon as possible.

Madame Epanchin now becomes furious with everyone. She tells Burdovsky that it is easy enough for him to refuse the Prince's money proudly because he knows it will be offered again. She also points out the falseness of their reasoning that they should feel no gratitude to the Prince because he is doing good just to ease his conscience. She says that if this is the case, the Prince should feel no gratitude to Pavlishtchev either. When the Prince admits that he will go to Burdovsky the next day, Madame Epanchin says that she does not want to see Myshkin again. Then she becomes incensed with Ippolit, who responds with a terrible coughing fit. Madame Epanchin becomes concerned about the boy and orders him to bed. However, Ippolit states he has only two weeks to live, and once he goes to bed, he will not get up again. Ippolit tells Madame Epanchin that he has been anxious to meet her, and wants to talk to her. He asks for tea, and Prince Myshkin invites everyone to stay for tea.

Comment: We learn the following facts:

1) **Burdovsky really thought he was Pavlishtchev's son.**

2) **Ippolit is dying of tuberculosis.**

PART II, CHAPTER 10

Ippolit tells Madame Epanchin that Lebedyev corrected Keller's article. Lebedyev says that he only corrected the first part, and Keller says that he got the "facts" from Lebedyev in return for six rubles. Lebedyev acts very contrite. Ippolit finds it very difficult to express himself and does not seem to be saying what he wants to say. He criticizes Madame Epanchin for being interested in what has been going on, and particularly for allowing her daughters to be present.

General Epanchin warmly defends his wife. Aglaia is most anxious to leave, but Madame Epanchin insists on staying for a little while, primarily because of her concern for Ippolit. She asks that Myshkin allow Ippolit to spend the night with him. Radomsky now enters the conversation and tells Ippolit that he seems to think he must uphold right even before finding out what is right. Radomsky concludes that this philosophy logically leads to a belief that might is right. Ippolit makes no reply, but listens to Radomsky with respect.

Ippolit becomes excited again and laughs as he invites everyone to his funeral. It is obvious that he is feverish, perhaps delirious. He tells Madame Epanchin that he came to Pavlovsk to see the trees. Then he comments that he is not quite eighteen. He starts talking about the thoughts he has at home while looking at the brick wall outside his bedroom window, but his speech is disconnected. Madame Epanchin is genuinely concerned about him and he realizes and appreciates her sympathy.

Ippolit complains that Nature is very fickle to give life and then take it away so quickly. Then he says that perhaps his early death is saving him from acting dishonorably. In the next breath, Ippolit declares, tragically, that he has done nothing and will leave nothing of himself for men to remember. This thought makes him break down and cry. Madame Epanchin tries to comfort him, and Ippolit asks her to take his brother and sisters away from his mother.

Comment: Madame Terentyev has been General Ivolgin's mistress. Ippolit does not approve, and thinks that her way of life will have a bad effect on his younger brother and sisters.

Madame Epanchin again asks her husband for advice. He declares that they should leave at once, giving Ippolit a chance to rest. Prince Myshkin, who appears ill himself, invites Ippolit and his friends to stay with him, but Ippolit indicates that he would prefer to return to St. Petersburg with them. Then he shouts that he hates all of them, particularly the Prince, whom he would like to murder.

This last outbreak proves too much for Madame Epanchin, who sarcastically thanks Prince Myshkin for his entertainment. The General also appears displeased and Aglaia demands that Myshkin get rid of the young men at once. Adelaida, Prince S. and Alexandra are more friendly, however, and Radomsky expresses his regret that the Prince has had so difficult an evening.

Ippolit and his friends finally leave. The Epanchins prepare to go also, but just as they leave the house, a carriage stops and one of the two well-dressed ladies in it speaks to Radomsky. She tells him not to worry because Rogozhin has paid certain IOUs for him. Radomsky declares his complete innocence and mystification, saying he does not know who the woman is, or anything about any IOUs. The Prince, who was startled at the sound of the woman's voice, seems extremely unwell.

Comment: As we can guess from Myshkin's reaction, the woman in the carriage is Nastasya Filippovna.

PART II, CHAPTER 11

The following day, Adelaida and Prince S. come to call on Prince Myshkin. From their conversation, the Prince deduces that Madame Epanchin is still quite angry with him. Just before they leave, Prince S. asks Myshkin about the incident of the woman in the carriage. Myshkin tells him that it was Nastasya, telling Radomsky not to worry about his debt to a moneylender. Prince S. says he does not understand this, because Radomsky is quite wealthy. He is also perplexed that Nastasya should act so familiarly toward Radomsky. Prince S. concludes that someone wants to blacken Radomsky's reputation.

Ganya tells the Prince that although Nastasya has been in Pavlovsk only four days, she already has attracted quite a following. Varya says that Radomsky has gone to St. Petersburg on business and that Ptitsyn is with him. She also comments that Aglaia has quarreled with her whole family.

Myshkin is very glad when he is alone at last. He wants very much to go back to Switzerland immediately, because he feels that if he does not, he will become so involved with this world that he will never be able to free himself. However, after very little hesitation, he decides he must stay because it would be cowardly to run away.

Comment: Here again we see Myshkin as a Christ-figure. The Prince would prefer a quiet, contemplative life, but knows that he has a mission in the world. He also realizes that he will never be happy.

In the late afternoon, Keller comes to see Myshkin. He declares that he did not accompany his friends back to the city because he wanted to tell the Prince the story of his life. However, without much preamble, he declares that he is so depraved that he has become a thief. He also confesses to many other sins, of which he seems almost proud. Myshkin declares his inability to believe Keller's tales and asks him why he has told these stories. Keller first says that he is attracted by the Prince's simplicity and then hesitates. Myshkin fills in the gap by asking if he wants to borrow money. Keller says that this is true, but asserts that he thought of borrowing money only after he planned his confession.

Myshkin tells Keller that he undoubtedly got both ideas at the same time. However he adds that Keller is not wicked because of this and confesses that he himself often has "double" thoughts.

Comment: The Prince's declaration that he often is troubled by good and evil ideas coming simultaneously reminds us that he is essentially one with Rogozhin.

The Prince tells Keller that if he gives him money, Keller will just drink more. Keller admits the truth of this and declares that to punish himself, he will ask for only twenty-five rubles, instead of one hundred fifty. The Prince gives him the money.

Just then Lebedyev comes in. As soon as Keller is gone, Lebedyev begins criticizing him. Myshkin says that Keller was really very sorry for his misdeeds, but Lebedyev says that words mean nothing. As an example, he refers to his abject apologies of the previous day which, he tells the Prince, were insincere. Myshkin asks him if he had anything to do with Nastasya's comments to Radomsky the day before. Lebedyev says that his only part was to tell Nastasya what people were with the Prince. At Myshkin's request, he begins to tell what he knows about the plot against Radomsky. However, he gets no further than a reference to Aglaia when the Prince interrupts and tells him to go away.

Comment: Radomsky is courting Aglaia Epanchin. From the various hints in the novel, we can guess that Nastasya is determined to prevent a marriage between Radomsky and Aglaia by making it appear that Radomsky is a spendthrift who associates with disreputable people.

Kolya comes in and tells the Prince that Aglaia has quarreled with her family over Ganya. Madame Epanchin has told Varya to stay away. Kolya says that he has suspected for some time that Ganya and Varya were plotting something, but he still does not know what it is. He goes on to say that although Ganya is vain and weak, he has some excellent points. Myshkin tells Kolya that Madame Epanchin must think Ganya dangerous, thus indicating that Ganya has received encouragement from Aglaia. Kolya is surprised at this, but then declares that he thinks Myshkin is jealous. The Prince blushes.

Comment: Aglaia has been favorably impressed by the change in Ganya. It appears that Varya has become friendly with the Epanchin girls primarily to do what she can to assist Ganya in his hopes of marrying Aglaia. Kolya's assumption that Myshkin is jealous appears justified by the Prince's embarrassment.

The following day, Myshkin is in St. Petersburg on business. On his way back to Pavlovsk, he meets General Epanchin, who asks him not to visit for a little while. However, the General is quite friendly. He explains that Radomsky may propose to Aglaia at any time, and that someone (Nastasya) is trying to prevent this from happening. The General cannot understand why Nastasya should want to interfere, unless she is trying to revenge herself on him. He adds that even this is mysterious, because he never injured her in any way. The General concludes that he is very apprehensive that some terrible trouble will befall them. Myshkin is very pleased that the General does not suspect him of being the cause of the plot against Radomsky.

Comment: This chapter gives us the following information:

1) Madame Epanchin is very angry with the Prince.

2) Lebedyev has had a hand in the "plot" against Radomsky.

3) Aglaia has quarreled with her family over Ganya.

4) Everyone is confused about the purpose of Nastasya's statement to Radomsky.

5) Although he does not admit it, the Prince knows why Nastasya is trying to degrade Radomsky.

PART II, CHAPTER 12

On the third day after the affair with "Pavlishtchev's son," Madame Epanchin comes to see the Prince. She begins by stating that it is all his fault. Then she comes straight to the point of her visit. She demands to know what the Prince wrote to Aglaia a few months before. The Prince tells her and declares that he wrote as a brother. Madame Epanchin asks him if he is in love with Aglaia and he denies it. Then she inquires if he is married to Nastasya. The Prince replies that he did not come to Russia to get married.

Comment: This remark again refers to the Prince's "mission."

Madame Epanchin also wants to know the meaning of the "poor knight" and of Nastasya's words to Radomsky. Myshkin denies any knowledge about either **episode**. Madame Epanchin declares that Aglaia will never marry either Myshkin or Radomsky and then asks the Prince if he knows that Ganya has been writing to Aglaia. This information comes as a surprise to Myshkin, but he is even more astonished when he learns that Aglaia has been writing to Nastasya as well.

Madame Epanchin now criticizes the Prince for not coming to see her. She interrupts his explanations by asking if he saw Burdovsky in St. Petersburg. Myshkin says that he did not, but has received a letter from "Pavlishtchev's son." He shows her the letter, in which Burdovsky declares his intention never to accept any money from him, and also thanks the Prince for helping his mother financially.

Madame Epanchin again becomes angry with Myshkin and tells him she never wants to see him again. The Prince tells her that Aglaia has already written a note to tell him not to visit them. Strangely enough, Madame Epanchin responds to this news by telling the Prince to come with her at once. She says that Aglaia wants someone like the Prince to laugh at, and probably wrote the note because she is angry that he has not come to visit.

Comment: In this last chapter of Part II, we learn:

1) **Aglaia has been corresponding with Ganya and with Nastasya.**

2) **Madame Epanchin does not want Aglaia to marry either Radomsky or the Prince.**

3) **The Prince has no plans to marry anyone.**

4) **Although Madame Epanchin denies it, she realizes that Aglaia loves the Prince.**

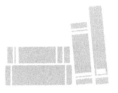

THE IDIOT

TEXTUAL ANALYSIS

PART III

PART III, CHAPTER 1

Comment: As is his custom, Dostoyevsky begins Part III with some introductory remarks. This chapter is composed of three distinct parts; all, however, have the same basic theme. The first part contains Dostoyevsky's observations on "men of affairs"; the second relates Madame Epanchin's thoughts about her family; and the third consists of a discussion of liberalism in Russia.

Dostoyevsky begins the chapter with a humorous discussion of the Russian civil service which, although large, seems totally incompetent. This leads to some remarks about the great value which is placed on lack of initiative and the disrespect accorded to men of genius.

This discussion, Dostoyevsky tells us, is intended to serve as an introduction to his comments on the Epanchin family.

Madame Epanchin worries constantly because she feels her family is different from others of the same social class. She is sure that this is her fault, and that because of her eccentricities, Alexandra and Aglaia will never get married.

Madame Epanchin's chief concern has always been Aglaia. What worries her most is that Aglaia is just like her. She uses words like "nihilist" and "eccentric" when describing Aglaia mentally, and is absolutely certain that her favorite daughter will be unhappy.

> **Comment: People of Madame Epanchin's generation seemed to call everything that young people did which was unusual or disapproved of, "nihilism." The situation is similar to that of calling all young men with beards "beatniks."**

Recently, Aglaia has pleased her mother by seeming more "normal," that is, taking a greater interest in social affairs; however, since Prince Myshkin's return, Aglaia has been quarrelsome and has acted strangely.

Dostoyevsky points out that these are Madame Epanchin's thoughts as she escorts Prince Myshkin to her summer villa. Madame Epanchin wonders to herself why she has confided so much in the Prince. She cannot understand why Aglaia should be so interested in him, and then reflects that she herself is vitally interested in him. She comes to the conclusion that she and her family are all eccentric and should be exhibited in glass cases.

By this time, Madame Epanchin and the Prince have arrived at the villa. The Prince sits pale and speechless, while Aglaia watches him intently. The family is in the middle of a discussion concerning liberalism. Radomsky maintains that the Russian liberal is un-Russian and hates Russia as well as despising her archaic institutions.

> **Comment: We may take this statement as containing the heart of Dostoyevsky's argument with the "Westernizers." The Westernizers, who called themselves Russian Liberals, admired European methods to the virtual exclusion of everything Russian. One of Dostoyevsky's chief complaints against liberals like Turgenev was that they despised Russia to the point of preferring to live abroad.**

Prince Myshkin, asked for his opinion, indicates that he thinks Radomsky is partly right. It soon appears, however, that Radomsky is not being serious, because he next asks the Prince what he thinks about a recent murder trial. The defense attorney, who seemed to feel that he was very liberal, said that the accused murderer of six people was so poor that it was natural for him to murder them. Prince Myshkin says that such perverted ideas are far more common than people think. He goes on to say that recently he visited some prisons and found that the criminals all felt that they had done wrong, even if they were unrepentant. However, the Prince continues, there is now a new breed of men who seem to feel that their criminal acts are morally right.

> **Comment: The Prince seems to be talking about nihilism.**

Radomsky appears very surprised and comments that Myshkin should have seen that Burdovsky and Doktorenko are nihilists.

At this point, Kolya mentions that Ippolit has arrived at Myshkin's villa. Radomsky makes some sarcastic remarks about Ippolit which Myshkin resents. Although Radomsky asserts that he is quite willing to forgive Ippolit, Myshkin says that this is not the point; Radomsky must be willing to receive forgiveness too. This statement is incomprehensible to Radomsky, even when Myshkin tries to explain by saying that Ippolit wants to bless everyone and be blessed by them in turn.

Prince S. tries to put matters right by telling Myshkin that achieving heaven on earth is more difficult than Myshkin, in his naivete, seems to think. Madame Epanchin, angry again, suggests that they all go and hear the band.

Comment: Prince S.'s comment to Myshkin is very perceptive. Myshkin indeed thinks that he will be able to induce people to base their actions on the principles of Christian love by setting a good example and by telling them what is right. However, Prince Myshkin is already beginning to realize the truth of Prince S.'s remark.

PART III, CHAPTER 2

Myshkin suddenly addresses Radomsky, saying he thinks well of him despite everything. Radomsky is extremely surprised and replies that he does not think the Prince meant to speak to him. Myshkin states that this is true, and compliments Radomsky on his intelligence in realizing that Myshkin's words are meant for someone else.

Comment: Myshkin's words really refer to Rogozhin.

Prince Myshkin then apologizes for his conduct of three days ago and says that he is going away very soon. Radomsky seems puzzled. Madame Epanchin is quite concerned and asks Kolya if

Myshkin's fits begin like this. The Prince reassures her and says that he knows that his illness, which has been present almost all his life, has left its mark upon him. He continues by saying he realizes he is out of place in society. If he spoke of his exalted ideas, Myshkin says, people would only laugh at him. Therefore, he will not mention them.

Comment: Prince Myshkin has realized that his mission will fail. He thinks that he is at fault and feels that if he were a better person, more in harmony with the ways of the world, people would listen to him. However, if he were more sophisticated, Myshkin probably would have no compulsion to reform the world.

Aglaia becomes very angry and asks Myshkin why he is saying all this to her family; she declares that he is far better than any of them, and criticizes him for having no pride. Kolya cheers for "the poor knight," and Aglaia, hysterical now, asks why everyone has been tormenting her for the past three days. She tells Myshkin that she will never marry him and asks how anyone could even consider marrying, him Then Myshkin tells Aglaia that he has not even asked her to marry him. This remark astounds Madame Epanchin. The Prince explains that it never occurred to him to propose to Aglaia, so that she has nothing to worry about.

Comment: Aglaia would not declare her intention of never marrying Myshkin if she were not in love with him. Thus, his protestations that he does not plan to ask her are not precisely tactful.

Myshkin looks so sincere and upset that Aglaia begins laughing at him. Her laughter is infectious, and soon everyone, including the Prince, is laughing merrily. Adelaida suggests that they all go for a walk and insists that Myshkin go with them. As they walk, Aglaia shows Myshkin a park bench where, she says pointedly, she often sits alone at seven o'clock in the morning.

The entire party arrives at the bandstand where a concert takes place every evening. A number of young men, most of them friends of Radomsky's, come up to pay their respects to the girls and their mother. They are particularly interested in Aglaia, who is sitting beside Myshkin. Prince Myshkin, however, seems totally unaware of his surroundings. He longs to be far away, alone, so that he can think. Finally, Aglaia asks him why he is staring at her in so strange a way; it makes her feel afraid of him. Myshkin does not answer, but seeing all the others laughing, he laughs too. This angers Aglaia, who mutters to herself, "idiot."

Nastasya enters the park with a noisy group of people. She comes toward the Epanchins, sees Radomsky, and tells him that his wealthy uncle has shot himself and that a large sum of government money is missing. A friend of Radomsky's says quite audibly that the "hussy" (Nastasya) should be whipped. Nastasya strikes him in the face with his own riding-whip. The insulted officer loses his self-control and lunges at Nastasya. However, at this crucial moment, Prince Myshkin grabs hold of the officer's arms and is himself pushed down. Keller steps forward to defend Nastasya, but the officer ignores him. By now, Rogozhin has taken Nastasya away, but not before he laughs at the officer. The officer assures himself of Myshkin's name and leaves, without listening to the Prince's protestations that Nastasya is insane.

Comment: The officer will ask Myshkin to fight a duel.

Comment (Additional): In this chapter we learn:

1) **Myshkin realizes that his "mission" is doomed to failure.**

2) Aglaia, by declaring that she will never marry the Prince, indicates that she loves him very much.

3) The "plot" against Radomsky continues; Nastasya tells him that his wealthy uncle has committed suicide and is suspected of embezzling large sums.

4) Myshkin, by preventing the officer from striking Nastasya, has offended him so deeply that a duel must result.

PART III, CHAPTER 3

Madame Epanchin is so dismayed at the scene in the public park that she almost runs home with her daughters. As far as she is concerned, Nastasya's remarks prove that Radomsky is a dissolute adventurer. As they reach their villa, they come upon General Epanchin, who has just returned from St. Petersburg. He looks very disturbed, asks for Radomsky, and whispers something to Prince S. No one notices Prince Myshkin, who has followed them to the house.

After a long time, Aglaia comes out of the house and sees Myshkin sitting alone on the porch. Aglaia asks him what he would do if someone challenged him to a duel. Myshkin seems perplexed and, in answer to her further questions, says that he would be afraid. However, he maintains that he is not a coward, because cowards run away. Since he says he has never fired a gun, Aglaia tells him what sort of a pistol to buy and how to load it. She advises that he practice shooting daily.

General Epanchin comes out to the verandah and tells Myshkin he must talk to him. As they walk toward Myshkin's villa, the General speaks in a disconnected manner. Myshkin, however, is not listening to him and does not realize that the General seeks information in a roundabout way. Finally, General Epanchin begins speaking of Nastasya. Myshkin says that she is mad, and the General states that he thought so too, at first. It appears that her latest statement to Radomsky is true, and General Epanchin suspects that her comment that Radomsky resigned his commission just in time is also true.

Comment: Radomsky's uncle, Kapiton Alexeyitch Radomsky, was very wealthy, and it was presumed that on his death Radomsky would inherit a large fortune. His uncle's suicide and apparent misappropriation of government funds would have forced Radomsky to resign his army commission if he had not done so already. The implication is that Radomsky had advance knowledge of his uncle's tangled affairs and resigned on that account.

The General assures Myshkin that Radomsky's personal fortune is intact. He then tells the Prince that Radomsky apparently proposed to Aglaia the previous month, and that she refused him. The General goes on to say that Aglaia has been laughing at all of them, particularly her mother, and has announced that Nastasya (whom she calls a madwoman) has decided that Aglaia and Myshkin must get married. To achieve her purpose, Nastasya has been working hard to blacken Radomsky's reputation.

Comment: We know that Aglaia's interpretation is correct. We know, too, that Prince Myshkin has suspected this all along. You will recall that at her birthday party (Part I, Chapter 16), Nastasya told Myshkin that he should marry Aglaia Epanchin.

After telling Prince Myshkin not to be angry because Aglaia is making fun of him, and assuring him that they all respect him deeply, the General says good-bye.

While the General has been talking, Prince Myshkin has been clenching his right fist. Now that he is alone, he opens it and reads the note Aglaia placed in his hand. In her note, Aglaia asks Myshkin to meet her the next morning at the park bench she pointed out to him. She says she has something very important to discuss with him.

Keller now comes up to the Prince to offer his services as a second.

Comment: The "second," who is a friend of the duelist, meets with the other man's second to arrange the time, place and method of the duel.

Prince Myshkin is astonished that he, too, should be talking of duels. Myshkin asserts that there is nothing to fight about; while he seized the officer's arms, the officer pushed him. Myshkin declares he is quite willing to apologize, but if the officer insists on a fight, he is ready. He tells Keller what Aglaia told him about loading guns. Then he invites Keller to have champagne with him. Keller is surprised at Myshkin's strange behavior and concludes that he must be feverish.

Myshkin says good-night to Keller and walks into the park. Scarcely aware of his surroundings, the Prince paces back and forth between the bench Aglaia pointed out to him and a particularly large tree. Finally, he sits down. He is in love with Aglaia, but he does not admit it to himself and would deny it if anyone accused him of being in love. He believes that she is making fun of him, but is not insulted. Happy that he will see her soon, he does not worry about what she may say to him.

Suddenly, Rogozhin appears. The Prince is surprised to see him. Rogozhin says that he came only because Nastasya is most anxious to see Myshkin. Rogozhin acknowledges that he has received a letter from the Prince, in which Myshkin asserts that he has forgiven Rogozhin and remembers only the "brother" with whom he exchanged crosses, not the man who tried to kill him. However, Rogozhin says that he still does not like Myshkin, and perhaps is not even sorry for trying to kill him.

Myshkin asserts that Rogozhin is insanely jealous over Nastasya, and that he could not repent of his murderous attack even if he wanted to. He adds that he suspected that Rogozhin would try to kill him. Then he tells Rogozhin that perhaps Nastasya torments him because she loves him so much. Rogozhin laughs and says that he has heard Myshkin is in the same predicament. Myshkin wonders at this and Rogozhin explains that Nastasya told him Myshkin loved Aglaia sometime before. Rogozhin confirms that Nastasya has told him that she will not marry him until Myshkin marries Aglaia. Myshkin reiterates his belief that Nastasya is insane, but Rogozhin asks why no one else has ever noticed it. He mentions that Nastasya has been writing to Aglaia. When Myshkin expresses his disbelief, Rogozhin laughs and says that the time may come when Myshkin, like Rogozhin, has spies telling him of everything Nastasya does.

Comment: Dostoyevsky apparently forgot that in Part II, Chapter 12, Madame Epanchin tells Myshkin that Aglaia and Nastasya are corresponding.

Myshkin suddenly realizes that it is his birthday. He invites Rogozhin to join him in some wine, and tells him that he is beginning a new life. Rogozhin says that he can see Myshkin is not his usual self.

Comment: Although the meaning of Myshkin's declaration that he is beginning a new life is not clear, we can guess, from what has gone on before, that Myshkin has decided to forget his "mission." He is in love with Aglaia, feels that she loves him, and realizes that his mission is doomed to failure. However, as we shall see, his attempt to live a "normal" life will also fail.

PART III, CHAPTER 4

As Myshkin and Rogozhin approach his villa, Myshkin notices with surprise that a number of his friends are gathered on the verandah, drinking champagne. He thinks it odd that they should have come, uninvited, to celebrate his birthday, especially since he just remembered the occasion himself.

Lebedyev tells the Prince that the gathering began quite by chance when Ippolit expressed the wish to wait for the Prince on the verandah. Burdovsky brought Ippolit, Lebedyev and his family joined them, Ganya and Ptitsyn happened to pass by, Keller and Ferdyshtchenko appeared, and finally Radomsky called. It seems that Keller's request for champagne was seconded by Kolya and readily complied with by Lebedyev. However, Lebedyev assures Myshkin that he has produced his own champagne and has set his daughter Vera to preparing refreshments.

Radomsky tells Myshkin that he wishes to speak to him privately. He tells the Prince that he has settled everything with

Kurmyshov (the officer whom Myshkin insulted), so that there will be no duel. Although he admits to Myshkin that he has something else to tell him, Radomsky says he will wait until the visitors have gone. Myshkin suggests that they go for a walk in the park, but Radomsky states he would rather wait, because he does not want anyone to know he has private business with the Prince.

Ippolit, despite his assurance that he feels uncommonly well, looks feverish. He has been drinking champagne, is overexcited and has talked a great deal, but said little that makes sense. Expressing regret that he has not brought the Prince a birthday present, Ippolit mysteriously hints that he has brought some kind of present. Suddenly, he asks when sunrise will occur and declares that he wishes to drink to the health of the sun as it rises.

> **Comment: Ippolit's "present," as we shall see in the next chapter, is a manuscript which he wants to read aloud. At this time of year, the days are so long at the latitude of St. Petersburg that it never really gets dark.**

The party now begins discussing Lebedyev's interpretation of the Apocalypse. Lebedyev vehemently expresses the opinion that the whole scientific and materialistic tendency of the last few centuries is leading to the ruination of mankind, because it has no moral basis. To explain what he means by a moral force binding men together, Lebedyev tells a story. He assures his listeners that what he says is factual.

During the Middle Ages, Lebedyev says, there were terrible famines every two or three years. Cannibalism was not infrequent. Lebedyev relates that one man confessed to having eaten sixty monks and six infants during the course of his long life. According to Lebedyev, the six infants represented an attempt on the part of the cannibal to change his ways and **refrain** from his sacrilegious culinary habits. He also makes the point that the cannibal must have been more afraid of his conscience than of any of the physical tortures which surely befell him to make this confession. Lebedyev concludes that mankind, while more prosperous now, is morally degenerate. Then, to prevent his listeners from bursting out angrily at him, Lebedyev ends by saying it is time for supper.

PART III, CHAPTER 5

Ippolit suddenly wakes up, and in distressed tones asks the Prince what time it is. He is relieved when Radomsky tells him he has slept less than ten minutes, but comments that Radomsky has been watching him closely all evening. Ippolit is in a feverish state of excitement. He shouts that Myshkin believes beauty will save the world because he is in love. Then, after acknowledging that he dislikes the Prince, he takes a large sealed envelope from his pocket and announces that he wishes to read a composition of his own aloud.

Everyone gathers around Ippolit, who comments that it is the seal, signifying mystery, which attracts them. After some preliminary hesitation about whether to read it or not, Ippolit begins to read his, "An Essential Explanation! Motto: Apres moi le deluge."

The narrative begins with an explanation of the time and circumstances of the writing. It was written the day and night before Ippolit came to Pavlovsk for the second time. He says that he wants to read it aloud at Pavlovsk, and does not intend to make any corrections. He insists that it will be wholly truthful, because someone who has only two weeks to live has no reason to lie. The manuscript is rambling. Among other things, Ippolit relates a nightmare about a poisonous scorpion. Then he hints that since it is not worthwhile to live only two weeks, he may as well kill himself. Describing various unfortunate people he has known, he says he despises them for remaining as poor as they are. Ippolit writes that there is no reason for anyone to remain poor and starving, that anyone with the gift of life should be able to become rich. As an example of his own predicament, Ippolit mentions that it is useless for him even to try to learn Greek, since he will die before he has time to master the grammar.

PART III, CHAPTER 6

Ippolit continues reading his "Explanation." Despite his assurance that he has no sympathy for unfortunate people, he tells a story which indicates that his actions can be quite different from his theories. Ippolit relates the circumstances under which he found, and was of considerable assistance to, a young physician and his family. When discussing this affair with a friend whom he had involved in the "act of charity," Ippolit commented that we give a little of ourselves with each act of kindness, thus becoming immortal, in a way. He concludes the story by saying that he really should not embark on a charitable work because he has so little time left to live that he could not conclude it. Ippolit continues his narrative with a description of his meeting with Rogozhin some ten days before. Rogozhin came to see him to obtain certain information, the nature of which Ippolit does not mention; he returned the visit the following day. Later that night, while lying in bed, he reflected on a painting at Rogozhin's house. Ippolit describes the painting, Holbein's "Descent from the Cross," in considerable detail. He wonders how, having seen this corpse, the Disciples could have believed that the Resurrection would occur.

Comment: This is the painting which so impressed Prince Myshkin (Part II, Chapter 4). Myshkin's conclusion, that such a painting could make one lose one's faith, is very similar to Ippolit's thoughts.

Then, Ippolit continues, he dreamed that someone showed him a large, repulsive spider and told him that this was the overwhelming force to which everything, even Christ, was subject. After that, Rogozhin seemed to come into his room. He sat and looked at him, without speaking, for nearly two hours. Ippolit writes that he was not sure whether the visitor was Rogozhin or a spirit, but the next morning he discovered that both his door and the street door were locked. Ippolit notes that this incident brought about his "final decision."

PART III, CHAPTER 7

Ippolit's reading continues with a description of a small pistol. He says that he decided to shoot himself at sunrise in Pavlovsk, and adds that the "Explanation" will clear things up for the police.

Comment: The "final decision" which Ippolit has referred to so often is his determination to commit suicide after reading his "Explanation" aloud.

One copy of the manuscript is to go to the Prince, the other to Aglaia Epanchin. Ippolit reflects that since he has only a few weeks to live, he can do anything he wants, including murder. However, he says that although no one has the right to judge him, he wishes to leave some defense of himself, in the form of his "Explanation." The remainder of Ippolit's manuscript consists of a discussion of his right to dispose of his remaining time as he wishes. He mentions that although he has tried not to believe in God, he has never succeeded. Adding that he should not be condemned for being unable to understand the mysterious ways of God, he concludes that perhaps suicide is the only action he has the time to finish.

Ippolit's listeners are quite angry by the time he finishes his reading. However, after he dramatically points out that the sun has risen, most of the guests ignore him or assert that he will not commit suicide. Lebedyev is sure that Ippolit will shoot himself and insists that the gun be handed over to him for safekeeping.

> **Comment: Lebedyev does not care whether Ippolit kills himself or not. However, he does not want any "regrettable" action to occur on his premises.**

Ippolit tells Kolya to get the gun out of his suitcase. Then he bids good-bye to Myshkin, takes a glass in his hand and runs off. Taking the pistol out of his pocket (where he has had it all this time), he presses it against his temple and pulls the trigger. It does not go off because it has not been primed. Everyone laughs, except Ippolit, who hysterically assures everyone that he really meant to kill himself. Finally, he faints. Keller announces that he will fight anyone who implies that Ippolit did not mean to commit suicide.

Most of the guests leave, rather hurriedly. Radomsky tells Myshkin that he has changed his mind and has decided to discuss his business with the Prince later on. He also assures the Prince that Ippolit will probably live for more than a month, if he does not surprise everyone by getting well. Although Radomsky feels Ippolit will not try to kill himself again, it is possible that he will murder someone.

Myshkin wanders off into the park and finally finds himself sitting on Aglaia's bench. He feels very unhappy and wishes he could go away. Suddenly, he thinks of Ippolit's analogy of the fly.

Ippolit wrote in his "Explanation" that he alone had no part in the general scheme; that even a fly had its purpose and place. Myshkin recalls his own feelings one day in Switzerland when he wept at the beauty of Nature in which he could have no part.

> **Comment: Ippolit feels like an outsider because he has so little time to live that he will never be able to accomplish anything. However, Ippolit, being only eighteen, does not know what he might be able to do if he had the time. Myshkin, on the other hand, has a distinct mission, but by now knows that he will never complete it successfully. His illness prevents him from carrying out his mission, and his mission hinders his efforts to become a part of the world.**

Myshkin falls asleep and dreams that a woman whom he knows well, but whose face indicates that she has committed a dreadful crime, beckons to him. She wishes to show him something in the park. Not wanting to acknowledge that she is a criminal, he nevertheless gets up to follow her, feeling that something terrible is about to happen. Just then, he is awakened by the sound of Aglaia laughing.

> **Comment: The woman in Myshkin's dream is obviously Nastasya.**

PART III, CHAPTER 8

Myshkin is at first surprised to see Aglaia. After she assures him that no one else has been there, and that he has been asleep, he comments that it is strange he should have such a dream at such a time.

Comment: Myshkin does not tell Aglaia about the dream. His feeling of foreboding during the dream about Nastasya, and his awakening to see Aglaia, indicate that the presentiment concerns his relationship with the two women.

Myshkin tells Aglaia about Ippolit's attempted suicide and his manuscript. Aglaia shows great interest and insists on hearing the entire story. She interrupts him frequently, seems very upset, and appears to be trying to warn the Prince of some unnamed danger. When Myshkin agrees with her that Ippolit probably wanted to kill himself so that she could read his "confession" afterward, she seems rather surprised. However, she warmly defends Ippolit, and says she will go to see him. Myshkin points out that he is not condemning Ippolit and sees nothing wrong with the youth's desire to have people respect him and beg him not to kill himself.

Finally, Aglaia comes to the point and asks Myshkin to be her friend. He looks at her intently; she blushes and becomes angry. The Prince assures her that her request is unnecessary. Aglaia tells the Prince that she respects both him and his mind.

Comment: Aglaia talks to Myshkin about two types of mind: one that matters, and one that does not. Apparently, Aglaia is differentiating between spiritual (or mystical) qualities and intellectual abilities. She feels that Myshkin's sensitivity is of utmost importance.

Aglaia comments that she is sure the Prince understands her meaning even though no one else, except her mother, does. She then tells Myshkin that she has refused to marry Radomsky and wants the Prince to help her run away from home. She complains that she is tired of wasting her time on social obligations and wants to go abroad, to travel and to study. She proposes that she and Myshkin set up a school for children, and tells him that if he refuses to help her, she will marry Ganya.

After saying that her family is always suspecting her of "things," she accuses Myshkin of thinking that she is in love with him and hopes to force him to marry her. He admits that he did fear, briefly, that she loved him. Aglaia becomes angry and refers to Myshkin's letter (Part II, Chapter 1) as a love-letter. Then she apologizes and says she knows that he wrote it at his most desolate moment, when he realized he could do nothing to help Nastasya. Suddenly, Aglaia says that she does not love Myshkin, but loves Ganya. She asserts that she has promised to marry him. When Myshkin expresses his disbelief, she alleges that Ganya burned his hand to prove his love.

Comment: When Aglaia admits that she "made up" the story about Ganya's having burned his hand for her, we wonder whether anything she says about Ganya is true.

Aglaia tells Myshkin that she knows everything about his relationship with Nastasya. For example, she knows that they lived together for a while and then Nastasya ran away with a landowner before going back to Rogozhin.

Comment: The events Aglaia speaks of occurred during the six-month period referred to in Part II, Chapter 1.

She states that Myshkin came to Pavlovsk because of Nastasya. Myshkin admits that this is true, but says he does not know what he can do for Nastasya. In answer to Aglaia's accusation, the Prince maintains that he does not love Nastasya, but only pities her. He explains that Nastasya thinks she is a "fallen woman" and some of her actions occur out of a compulsion to prove her degraded character to herself and to others.

Comment: Myshkin is quite correct about Nastasya's motivation. All through the book she is trying to punish herself for her supposedly "sinful" life.

Then Aglaia tells Myshkin about the letters Nastasya has written to her. She says they are the letters of an insane woman. Nastasya writes that she loves Aglaia and urges her to marry Myshkin. However, Aglaia feels that if she and Myshkin are married, Nastasya will kill herself, and therefore it would be better for him to sacrifice himself for Nastasya. Prince Myshkin says that he cannot, although he wanted to once, because he knows that Nastasya will be doomed with him. He comments that he should not have come for three years, but came because of Nastasya.

Comment: In three years, Myshkin will be thirty years old. He feels that he would be better prepared to carry out his mission at that time. It is interesting to note that Christ began his ministry at the age of thirty, and that Myshkin's physical appearance (Part I, Chapter 1) is similar to that of Christ as portrayed in Russian icons.

After this, Aglaia becomes furious and tells Myshkin that Nastasya must stop writing letters to her. At that moment, Madame Epanchin appears and asks what is going on. Aglaia screams that she will marry Ganya and runs home. Madame Epanchin asks Myshkin to account for what has been going on.

Comment: This chapter, consisting of Myshkin's conversation with Aglaia, tells us the following facts:

1) Aglaia wants to go abroad with Myshkin and found a school.

2) Aglaia says she loves Ganya and will marry him.

3) Aglaia knows quite a lot about Myshkin's relationship with Nastasya.

4) Nastasya loves both Aglaia and Myshkin and wants them to marry. However, she will probably commit suicide if they do.

5) Myshkin acknowledges that he came to Pavlovsk for Nastasya's sake, but cannot help her.

6) Myshkin realizes that because of his involvement with Nastasya, he has not had sufficient time to prepare himself for carrying out his mission.

PART III, CHAPTER 9

Myshkin explains his meeting with Aglaia to her mother and then returns to his villa. Kolya reports that Ippolit is sleeping soundly, and comments on how impressed he was by his friend's "Explanation." Then Lebedyev comes in to tell the Prince that four hundred rubles have been stolen from his coat pocket. He says that he suspects Ferdyshtchenko of the theft, because Ferdyshtchenko spent the night there but mysteriously left early in the morning.

Comment: Ferdyshtchenko turned up at Myshkin's birthday celebration in Keller's company.

Lebedyev talks at great length concerning his suspicions of Ferdyshtchenko, and constantly asserts that no one else could have committed the crime. However, he speaks strangely, making several unclear references to General Ivolgin, until finally Prince Myshkin is thoroughly confused.

Comment: Lebedyev's odd way of speaking is completely consistent with his usual method of saying one thing while hinting another. In this instance, Lebedyev is implying that General Ivolgin is responsible for the theft.

PART III, CHAPTER 10

It is not until evening that Myshkin finally forces himself to read Nastasya's letters to Aglaia. They have a nightmarish quality, but nevertheless Myshkin feels that there is something true in them.

Comment: Dostoyevsky notes here that sometimes, when we wake from a nightmare, we have the feeling that during the dream we realized something of vital importance which we can no longer recall. Dostoyevsky, in this comment on the nature of dreams, foreshadows the work of the pioneer psychologist, Sigmund Freud (1865–1939).

As Aglaia said, Nastasya writes of her love for Aglaia. She dwells on Aglaia's perfection, and her own degradation. At one point, Nastasya writes that to her, Myshkin and Aglaia are one.

> **Comment: Myshkin and Aglaia, who, to Nastasya, embody good, seem identical for that reason.**

Nastasya also writes that while most people cannot love anyone besides themselves, Aglaia is so far above everyone else that, for Myshkin's sake, she can truly love all mankind. Nastasya describes a picture she invented, of Christ sitting alone, except for a little child.

> **Comment: It is obvious that Nastasya identifies Myshkin with Christ, and Aglaia with the child.**

Nastasya writes of Rogozhin, whose eyes gaze at her even when he is not present. She says she knows that he loves her so much that he hates her, and that he will kill her.

> **Comment: Rogozhin's eyes, which seem disembodied, terrify Nastasya just as they disturbed Myshkin. In them, Nastasya seems to discover the fate which awaits her. Nastasya's comment that Rogozhin loves her so much that he hates her recalls Myshkin's statement (Part II, Chapter 3) that Rogozhin's love and hate are identical.**

After reading the letters, which fill him with foreboding, Myshkin wanders in the park for a long time. Finally, he finds himself near the Epanchin's villa. He goes in, but sees no one until Alexandra comes into the room with a candle. She seems surprised to see him, and finally tells him that it is after midnight.

Returning to the park, Myshkin seems to have the same dream of Nastasya standing before him. This time, however, it is not a dream. As in his dreams, she kneels and cries, begging him to tell her if he is happy or not. She promises to go away the next day and says she will never see him again. Rogozhin appears, takes her to her carriage and returns to Myshkin. Myshkin has apparently written to Rogozhin, asking him to take Nastasya away, and to prevent her from writing to Aglaia again. Rogozhin knows the content of Nastasya's letters. When Myshkin says that she is insane, Rogozhin almost whispers that perhaps she is not.

Comment: In one of her letters, Nastasya writes that she knows Rogozhin has a razor which he will use to kill her. Rogozhin knows that her remarks about the razor are not delusions; her conviction that he will murder her is justified, even if the weapon will be different.

Rogozhin tells Myshkin that he is going away with Nastasya. As he leaves, he asks Myshkin why he did not answer Nastasya's question when she asked if he is happy. When Myshkin says he is not, Rogozhin laughs.

Comment: Rogozhin knows that the Prince could not possibly be happy. He seems to derive considerable pleasure from Myshkin's deep unhappiness, partly because he is largely responsible. As Myshkin himself indicated (Part III, Chapter 9), he is not ready to undertake his mission, but has been drawn into the world because of Rogozhin and Nastasya. The Prince feels that it is his duty to try and "save" Nastasya; Rogozhin knows that this is impossible and has been doing all in his power to thwart Myshkin's efforts.

THE IDIOT

PART IV, CHAPTER 1

Dostoyevsky begins this chapter with an amusing discussion of "ordinary" characters. These are, he says, very hard to describe and frequently do not appear in novels. However, Dostoyevsky notes that "ordinary" people, who are after all in the majority, must be dealt with somehow. As an example, he mentions Varvara Ptitsyn, her husband, and her brother Ganya Ivolgin. Dostoyevsky goes on to say that unintelligent people do not mind being "ordinary," although the intelligent person of good family and excellent education resents his lack of originality.

Dostoyevsky tells us that Ptitsyn is fairly content with his lot; he does not have unreasonable ambitions and will be quite happy with the modest fortune he will undoubtedly amass. Varya too has adjusted well to her circumstances. However, Ganya really feels bad at his inability to do anything to set himself apart from the majority of men. He know that to "get ahead" he has to be really mean. Unfortunately, he can never carry out his intentions. Thus, he loses his chance to marry Nastasya and cannot even accept the small fortune she derisively throws at him.

After this introductory explanation of three "ordinary" characters, Dostoyevsky continues the story line of *The Idiot*. A week has elapsed since the events related in the last chapter of Part III. Varya, returning to her Pavlovsk cottage from a visit to the Epanchins, finds the household in an uproar. Ganya and his father are shouting at each other. Varya tells Ganya that Prince Myshkin is unofficially engaged to Aglaia. The Epanchins are having a party, to which Byelokonsky has been invited, and at which the engagement probably will be announced.

Comment: At first, Varya says that the engagement is formal, and that Aglaia has consented. Later on, she says that Aglaia has not made a definite commitment.

The conversation of the brother and sister returns to the subject of their father. Apparently, General Ivolgin has called on the Epanchins, made inquiries about possible employment, and complained bitterly about his treatment at the hands of Ganya and the rest of his family. Ganya is beside himself with rage, and keeps harping on the fact that his father is a thief and a drunkard. He refers to the fact that even though Prince Myshkin and Lebedyev have tried to keep the matter secret, news of the "scandal" has leaked out, presumably through Ippolit.

Comment: Although neither Ganya nor Varya mentions the facts of the incident, it is apparent that they are referring to General Ivolgin's theft of four hundred rubles from Lebedyev. You will recall that in Part III, Chapter 9, Lebedyev told Prince Myshkin that

someone had stolen money from him. Lebedyev, while
stating that he suspected Ferdyshtchenko of the theft,
implied that General Ivolgin was responsible for it.

Ganya and Varya then begin discussing Ippolit, who has come
to stay at Ptitsyn's home. Ganya is incensed with the boy, whom
he calls a trouble-maker. He has little sympathy for Ippolit, and
seems rather angry that he has not died yet. The shouting becomes
louder, and finally General Ivolgin enters the room in an absolute
fury. Ptitsyn, Madame Ivolgin, Kolya and Ippolit follow him.

PART IV, CHAPTER 2

Ippolit has been staying at Ptitsyn's for about five days. Actually,
it was Ganya who suggested the move, but Ippolit has shown
no gratitude toward him, and in fact has been making unkind
remarks to Ganya ever since. It is against Ippolit in particular
that General Ivolgin directs his anger. Although it is not clear
what Ippolit has done or said, it appears that he has been
needling the General about a certain Kapiton Eropyegov. Ganya
interjects that Eropyegov never existed. This infuriates General
Ivolgin, who apparently has been telling Ippolit tall tales about
this non-existent gentleman. Finally, General Ivolgin announces
that he cannot stay another night in this house where everyone
insults him. He orders Kolya to get his suitcase and storms out
of the room.

Comment: During the argument with his father,
Ganya has hinted at the "disgrace" which has fallen
on the family through his father's actions. He is,
of course, referring to the theft. Neither Madame

Ivolgin nor Kolya knows of this incident, and Varya and Ganya have been trying to keep it from them.

Ganya now turns on Ippolit, reminding him that he is a guest and should speak more civilly. Ippolit retorts that Ganya is also a guest. Then he says that he is going to stay with his mother, who has rented rooms in Pavlovsk, but before he leaves, he wishes to make Ganya well aware of his hatred for him. He tells Ganya that he is anxious to degrade him purely because Ganya is such an ordinary person. He taunts Ganya with having no originality, and yet thinking of himself as terribly intelligent.

Comment: Ipppolit echoes Dostoyevsky's words in Part IV, Chapter 1, about Ganya's commonness. Of course, being told that he is just like everyone else is the worst blow to Ganya's pride.

Ippolit goes on to tell Ganya that he will not gain the affection of "a certain lady." Both Ganya and Varya immediately realize that Ippolit is referring to Aglaia Epanchin. However, Ganya does not feel that Ippolit's prediction will come true, and as soon as the boy leaves the room, he triumphantly shows Varya a note from Aglaia asking them to meet her in the park the next morning. Aglaia says she wishes to ask their advice about an important matter. Feeling quite pleased, Ganya thinks that he still has a chance to marry Aglaia.

There is another commotion, this time the noise and bustle connected with General Ivolgin's departure. Although the family is most anxious to avoid a scandal, the General does not seem to care what the neighbors think. When he gets into the street, he curses the household.

PART IV, CHAPTER 3

Comment: This chapter and the next two and a half chapters are, in a way, "flashbacks." Dostoyevsky will elaborate on the various matters referred to in Chapters 1 and 2.

After informing Myshkin of the theft of four hundred rubles, Lebedyev completely avoids him for three days. General Ivolgin also acts strangely. He and Lebedyev spend most of their time together, drinking, singing and quarreling. The morning after a particularly violent quarrel, the General tells Prince Myshkin that he wants to ask his advice about a very important matter. Although he talks for quite a while, General Ivolgin does not come to the point. However, he disturbs Myshkin who readily assents to see him again the following day. Immediately after the General's departure, Myshkin asks Lebedyev to come and see him.

Myshkin finally gets Lebedyev to talk about the missing four hundred rubles. Lebedyev tells the Prince that he found them several days ago. When Prince Myshkin asks how General Ivolgin reacted to the discovery, Lebedyev tells him, at great length, that he found the money but pretended he had not found it and left it so the General could find it. However, General Ivolgin has been strangely unobservant. Finally, Myshkin asks Lebedyev why he is torturing his old friend. Acting surprised, Lebedyev protests that he has never loved the General more than he does now. He gives the money to Myshkin, asking him to keep it for a short while, and says he will surely "find" it soon.

Comment: Prince Myshkin may be confused at Lebedyev's little plot, but it is obvious to us that Lebedyev, knowing that the General took the money originally, is playing a cruel little "game." Instead of

regarding the incident as a temporary indiscretion on the part of General Ivolgin, as anyone else would, Lebedyev is putting the old man through a great deal of mental torture. Lebedyev is being truthful when he says he has the highest regard for the General; with his ambivalent personality, he enjoys torturing people and "likes" them because he can torture them.

PART IV, CHAPTER 4

The next day, General Ivolgin tells Prince Myshkin that he has broken completely with Lebedyev and will leave his house immediately. He tells the Prince that he cannot be friendly with a man who tells outrageous lies. Lebedyev has told the General that he has a wooden leg, having had one leg shot off in 1812. Prince Myshkin interjects that Lebedyev certainly is not old enough to have had this misfortune happen to him. General Ivolgin agrees that the story is obviously false, and says that Lebedyev made it up because he does not believe that the General was one of Napoleon's pages in 1812.

Comment: Napoleon Bonaparte's invasion of Russia in 1812 ended with the complete victory of Russia. There is some doubt as to whether the French could have been defeated so completely had the Russian winter not been so early and severe as it was in that year. In any event, Russians of Dostoyevsky's era still looked back on the campaign of 1812 as one of the proudest moments in their history.

General Ivolgin then proceeds to tell Prince Myshkin about his experiences as one of Napoleon's pages in 1812. He begins by saying that he was ten or eleven years old at that time, and that he looks much younger than he really is. The story is quite fantastic; according to General Ivolgin, it was he who advised Napoleon to order the retreat from Moscow.

Comment: General Ivolgin has outdone himself in this remarkable tale. Apparently, he almost believes that all these things happened to him. The old man is deeply hurt because Lebedyev has been making fun of him by telling an equally fantastic story.

General Ivolgin leaves Myshkin quite pleased at his success, for Myshkin has acted as though he believes the General's story. However, Myshkin is afraid that the General will eventually feel insulted at Myshkin's pretense of belief. This is in fact what occurs.

The General, having left Lebedyev's, goes to Ptitsyn's home where he argues with everyone. Kolya follows him into the street and keeps asking his father what is wrong, and why he is acting so strangely. General Ivolgin does act quite oddly, starting sentences but never finishing them. Finally, Kolya finds out what is wrong: General Ivolgin has a stroke.

PART IV, CHAPTER 5

Comment: In this chapter, Dostoyevsky explains how the "engagement" between Aglaia and Myshkin occurred. He begins by noting that Varya's statement that there was a formal engagement was exaggerated.

It has suddenly occurred to the Epanchins that Aglaia is in love with Prince Myshkin. However, she denies it. Madame Epanchin, who, of course, worries more than the rest of her family, is not at all comforted by Princess Byelokonsky's assurance that she is jumping to unwarranted conclusions. Returning home, Madame Epanchin finds that Aglaia has confused everyone still further by first quarreling with Prince Myshkin and then sending him, through Kolya, the gift of a hedgehog. No one seems to understand the symbolism of the hedgehog and everyone except General Epanchin suspects that there is deep meaning in the gift. Myshkin understands Aglaia's gift to mean merely that she respects him and is sorry for having ridiculed him.

Comment: Whatever we may think about the symbolism of the hedgehog (for instance, it has a prickly exterior but is soft and vulnerable inside, like Aglaia herself), Dostoyevsky tells us that General Epanchin is correct in surmising that the gift has no hidden meaning.

When Myshkin calls on the Epanchins that evening, Aglaia imperiously demands that he explain what he thinks the hedgehog means. Prince Myshkin stammers, blushes, and is unable to make a coherent reply. Then she further surprises everyone by asking him whether he is proposing marriage to her or not. He answers affirmatively, to the intense dismay of both General and Madame Epanchin. Aglaia next asks Myshkin his financial status. As his fortune is really quite small she asks if he intends to enter government service. Myshkin replies that he hopes to become a private tutor.

Comment: Aglaia's questions are highly improper. Traditionally, her father should privately ask Prince Myshkin about his "prospects."

Finally, Aglaia's sisters cannot help laughing. Aglaia laughs too and runs out of the room. Soon Myshkin is left alone with

General Epanchin, who is quite confused and does not know whether Aglaia is serious about the Prince or not. He is called away by his family and finds Aglaia laughing and crying at the same time. Everyone assumes that Aglaia loves Myshkin, although she angrily denies it. At the urging of her mother, she goes to apologize to the Prince. As soon as she has left the room, the General asks his family to explain what is going on. Madame Epanchin says that Aglaia will undoubtedly marry Myshkin.

Aglaia apologizes to Prince Myshkin with great sincerity, telling him that she is foolish and that of course the incident can have no real significance. At this moment the rest of her family comes in. Myshkin, however, is extremely happy and spends the rest of the evening talking to the Epanchins.

During the next few days, Aglaia quarrels repeatedly with Prince Myshkin. However, he remains in excellent spirits, so much so that Ippolit makes a point of warning him about his "rival" Ganya. Ippolit bitterly remarks that everyone is angry with him, because instead of dying he seems to be getting better.

Comment: Dostoyevsky comments that as is so often the case with people dying of tuberculosis, Ippolit really thinks he is much improved. Dostoyevsky's first wife died of tuberculosis and he was well acquainted with the states of mind of cases of this nature.

PART IV, CHAPTER 6

Dostoyevsky tells us that Varya has also exaggerated the importance of the Epanchin's party. It is true that Princess Byelokonsky will be there, but the party is to be quite small. It is not intended as an engagement party, but rather as a means to introduce Prince Myshkin to "society." The Epanchins are really not sure what purpose the gathering is to serve, but they hope to gain the old Princess's approval in case Myshkin and Aglaia should marry.

They are all quite concerned about the impression Myshkin will make on those invited to the party. Prince Myshkin is aware of their nervousness, but does not feel particularly anxious himself. However, the day before the scheduled event Aglaia tells him quite seriously that he will undoubtedly talk too much and will probably break a valuable Chinese vase by which her mother sets great store. Prince Myshkin says that he will try his best to say nothing at all, and will sit as far from the vase as possible. Aglaia's words make a deep impression on him and he sleeps very badly.

Early on the day of the party, Lebedyev comes to see the Prince. He is already drunk and talks quite incoherently. The gist of his conversation is that he has been writing anonymously to Madame Epanchin and has already called on her to give her a letter written by Aglaia to Ganya. He does not mention how the message came into his possession. Madame Epanchin, instead of thanking him for his interest, gave him back the letter unopened and turned him out of her house.

Lebedyev gives Myshkin the letter with the suggestion that he open it. Myshkin is, of course, shocked at this idea. Finally the Prince gives the letter to Kolya, telling him to hand it to his brother as if it came directly from Aglaia.

Comment: This is the letter referred to in Part IV, Chapter 2, in which Aglaia asked Ganya and Varya to meet her.

Soon after this, the news comes that General Ivolgin has suffered a stroke. Myshkin spends most of the remainder of the day at Ptitsyn's, where the General has been taken.

> **Comment: At this point Dostoyevsky, having satisfied our curiosity about various matters, continues with the plot of *The Idiot*. It is quite probable that his "flashback" was not so much a literary device as a method of making the novel longer. He was paid by the page, after all.**

That evening, Myshkin makes a favorable first impression on the Epanchin's guests. He in his turn is quite pleased with his entrance into "society." He does not realize that the "charming" people who are gathered at the Epanchins' are anything but wise, witty and gracious. Dostoyevsky tells us that the guests are, for the most part, rather ordinary people who have nothing but their money and their high social position to recommend them. However, they all feel that they are honoring the Epanchins by coming.

> **Comment: Dostoyevsky satirizes the guests by showing them is completely self-centered. Each is individualized by some amusing eccentricity, for example, the "elderly anglomaniac," Ivan Petrovitch.**

Gradually Prince Myshkin begins to feel more at ease. For a while he sits quietly, listening happily to the conversation, but finally he begins to talk.

PART IV, CHAPTER 7

Prince Myshkin joins the conversation when he hears the name of his patron, Pavlishtchev, mentioned. The speaker, Ivan

Petrovitch, was related to Pavlishtchev and recalls having met Myshkin when he was a boy. Myshkin expresses great surprise at meeting a relative of Pavlishtchev's, and only makes himself seem more uncouth by trying to explain why he is so surprised.

A man identified only as the "old dignitary" remarks that Pavlishtchev was heavily influenced by a Jesuit priest. Ivan Petrovitch confirms this, saying that Pavlishtchev became a Roman Catholic shortly before his death. Prince Myshkin is astounded, and asks how Pavlishtchev, who was a good Christian, could have embraced the Roman Catholic faith. He asserts passionately that Roman Catholicism is "unchristian."

The mention of his benefactor seems to have launched the Prince on a heated defense of his philosophy. He maintains that both atheism and socialism have originated in an effort to fill the moral vacuum created by Roman Catholicism's failure to uphold the Christian ideal. He goes on to say that Russians have much work to do; that they must "save" Europe from the evils of atheism and socialism and lead the Europeans back to the truths of Christianity.

Comment: Here Myshkin is preaching his "mission." He feels that he must convince the Russians, particularly those in high social and economic positions, of their duty to the rest of mankind. Russia must "save" the rest of the world, bringing it back to the one "true" Church, which is, of course, the Russian Orthodox Church.

In Part III, Chapter 3, Myshkin told Rogozhin that he was beginning a new life. Presumably, he was giving up his "mission." However, he has not been able to forget it entirely.

Myshkin notes that Russians feel the spiritual void more than Europeans. They therefore go to extremes, becoming either violently religious or violently atheistic. He feels that Russians would become gentle and philosophical if the Russian Christ were preached to them.

Comment: Dostoyevsky is, through Myshkin, expressing his own religious philosophy. To Dostoyevsky, the Russian Christ is the true one, but has been forgotten by all but a few. What is wrong with the world could be set right by a return to Christian principles (not necessarily a return to a particular form of organized religion). Myshkin's speech was foreshadowed by the "parables" with which he answered Rogozhin's question about his belief in God (Part II, Chapter 4).

In the middle of his emotional outburst, Myshkin gets up, gesticulates wildly, and as Aglaia predicted, breaks the valuable Chinese vase.

Comment: At the beginning of the party Myshkin sat as far away from the vase as possible, but gradually moved closer to it as his interest in the conversation increased. Aglaia had particularly warned him about this vase and Myshkin had a presentiment that he would break it. The breaking of the vase which as a material possession may represent the world, possibly symbolizes the incompatibility of Myshkin's philosophy with the modern materialistic world.

Myshkin is of course aghast at what he has done. However, much to his surprise, everyone begins laughing in a friendly manner, and all, including Madame Epanchin, urge him not to be concerned. Feeling at ease once more, Myshkin continues his "lecture" on the role of the Russian in world civilization. He tells everyone that he has heard much that is bad about the Russian nobility but finds, on this his first introduction to it, that it is not decadent. He again becomes terribly excited and finally suffers an epileptic attack.

After Myshkin's seizure, the guests soon leave. Madame Epanchin decides that Myshkin certainly will not be a suitable husband for Aglaia. However, the following day, when Aglaia tells her sisters that Myshkin means nothing at all to her, Madame Epanchin surprises everyone, including herself, by passionately criticizing Aglaia for her harsh words.

Comment: Dostoyevsky ends the chapter by stating that Madame Epanchin is unjust to her daughter. He hints that Aglaia has decided to marry Prince Myshkin.

PART IV, CHAPTER 8

Prince Myshkin's epileptic attack is relatively mild, and the next morning he feels fairly well, although very depressed. Kolya comes to see him and asks the Prince to explain General Ivolgin's strange affairs to him. The boy is naturally deeply distressed on learning that his father has been a thief, but Myshkin comforts him by telling him that the old general has such a noble character that he has suffered a stroke as a result of his remorse over his action.

Madame Epanchin, her daughters, and Prince S. come to call on the Prince early in the afternoon. They inquire after his health, urge him to forget the incident at the party, and tell him to visit them as soon as he feels well again. After they leave, Prince Myshkin is even more depressed, because Aglaia has said nothing to him. Then, however, Vera Lebedyev gives him a verbal message from Aglaia. Aglaia asks him to remain at home until early in the evening. Soon after this, Ippolit comes in. He is coughing harder and feels he really will die very soon. It is from Ippolit that Myshkin learns the purpose of Aglaia's directions to him. Ippolit has been in communication with Aglaia, Nastasya and Rogozhin. Through him, Aglaia has arranged a meeting with Nastasya, to take place that evening at Darya Alexeyevna's house in Pavlovsk. Myshkin presumably will escort Aglaia there. Ippolit adds that he met Aglaia by appointment that morning and witnessed a meeting between Aglaia, Ganya and Varya. Aglaia told them that she appreciated their friendship and then dismissed them.

Comment: This was the meeting Ganya was looking forward to. He had hoped it would turn out differently.

Finally evening comes. Myshkin is ready when Aglaia calls for him and they go to Darya Alexeyevna's without speaking. Rogozhin opens the door for them and tells them that the house is empty except for the four of them. Aglaia and Nastasya hardly look at each other and no one speaks for some minutes. Then Aglaia tells Nastasya that she has asked to meet her in order to answer her letters in person. She states that she loves Myshkin and that Nastasya does not. Adding that Nastasya is incapable of loving anyone or anything except her own shame, she asks Nastasya to go away and leave Myshkin in peace.

Comment: Aglaia's comment that Nastasya loves only the thought of her own humiliation is very perceptive. Prince Myshkin, of course, recognized this almost immediately. As he told Aglaia (Part III,

Chapter 8), he has tried to restore Nastasya's self-confidence without success.

The discussion between Aglaia and Nastasya becomes bitter and Aglaia comments that Nastasya should have become a "washerwoman."

Comment: At her birthday party (Part I, Chapter 16), Nastasya vowed that she would either run away with Rogozhin or become a "washerwoman." This is a polite synonym for prostitute.

Aglaia also remarks that Nastasya does not want to marry Rogozhin, because if she does she will no longer be able to take pride in her degraded condition.

At last Nastasya ends her silence by claiming that Prince Myshkin loves her more than he does Aglaia. Nastasya proudly asserts that if she reminds Myshkin of his promise, he will leave Aglaia forever. Aglaia is obviously afraid that this will happen. Telling Rogozhin to go away, Nastasya hysterically points to Myshkin and cries that if he does not come to her immediately, Aglaia can have him. Myshkin hesitates for a moment and Aglaia runs out of the house. Although he tries to follow her, Nastasya clutches at him and then faints.

When she regains consciousness, Nastasya again tells Rogozhin to go away. He does, and Myshkin is left with Nastasya, whom he tries to calm by stroking her face as though she were a child.

Comment: Myshkin treats Nastasya as a child, as indeed she is in many ways. Rather than loving her, he pities her as he would an unfortunate child.

The scene between Myshkin, Aglaia, Nastasya and Rogozhin represents one of the dramatic high points of the novel. Myshkin is finally forced to make a choice between the two women. He hesitates for a moment, but we know that he will abide by his final decision. Although he obviously would prefer to go to Aglaia, he feels that Nastasya needs him more than Aglaia does. Unfortunately, he also knows that he will not be able to help Nastasya.

PART IV, CHAPTER 9

Dostoyevsky tells us that two weeks have elapsed since the dramatic confrontation between Aglaia and Nastasya. He mentions various rumors which have flown around Pavlovsk concerning a wealthy nobleman's public repudiation of his engagement to a respectable girl of good family. The most popular rumor states that the nobleman jilted his fiancée, whom he loved, simply to prove his nihilistic philosophy by marrying a woman of ill repute. Following his summary of these fantastic stories, Dostoyevsky notes that the true state of affairs is hardly more believable than the gossip.

Prince Myshkin, we learn, is to marry Nastasya in a very short time. He has turned arrangements for the wedding over to Lebedyev, Keller and a few others, and seems to have no concern over his approaching marriage. He spends most of his time with Nastasya, and seems uneasy if he is away from her for very long at a time. However, he frequently calls on the Epanchins although they refuse to receive him and will not permit him to see Aglaia.

Almost everyone connected with the Epanchins also snubs Prince Myshkin. Radomsky, however, maintains friendly relations with the Prince, and it is through him that Myshkin learns that Aglaia has been quite ill. She has finally recovered and the entire family has moved to their country estate. They plan to go abroad in the autumn, immediately after Adelaida's marriage to Prince S.

Radomsky asks Prince Myshkin how he could have treated Aglaia so badly, and how he can contemplate marrying Nastasya. Trying to explain his complicated feelings and motives, Myshkin emphasizes the fact that his marriage to Nastasya does not matter. He keeps repeating that Aglaia will understand, if only he has the opportunity to explain matters to her.

Puzzled, Radomsky proceeds to analyze Prince Myshkin's motives. Noting that the Prince came from Switzerland without any experience of the world, and that he was terribly tired and over-excited during his first day in St. Petersburg, Radomsky says that Myshkin, filled with idealistic fervor, thought he saw, in Nastasya, a way of putting his ideals into practice. Myshkin agrees with this description of his aims on first coming to Russia, and blames himself for causing Aglaia pain. However, Myshkin maintains that he still does not understand why Aglaia ran off, and why he is not permitted to see her. Radomsky very carefully explains that Aglaia saw that he loved Nastasya and wanted to marry her. Myshkin protests that he does not love Nastasya, that he is, in fact, afraid of her, but that he could not desert her because she would kill herself if he did.

Radomsky concludes by saying that he does not think Myshkin loves either of the women. When he leaves, however, he is still puzzled and wonders how it is possible to love two women at the same time, with quite different kinds of love.

Comment: As Dostoyevsky notes, Radomsky's analysis of Prince Myshkin is psychologically sound.

Prince Myshkin is not concerned about his forthcoming marriage to Nastasya and can state, quite truthfully, that it does not matter because he realizes that Nastasya will back down at the last moment. He does love the two women with different kinds of love: Nastasya he pities and considers child-like; Aglaia he loves as a spiritual equal.

PART IV, CHAPTER 10

General Ivolgin dies of a second stroke, occurring some eight days after the first. At the funeral Myshkin is again conscious of Rogozhin's intent stare and finds out, from Lebedyev, that he has been staying in Pavlovsk. At the suggestion of Kolya, Myshkin asks Keller and Burdovsky to be his attendants at the wedding.

Everyone at Pavlovsk talks about the forthcoming wedding of Myshkin and Nastasya. Although Myshkin's friends, particularly Madame Ivolgin, suggest that the wedding be held privately, Myshkin replies that Nastasya especially wishes it to be public.

Keller, pleased at being asked to take part in the wedding, offers the Prince his services as a boxer, should they become necessary. He tells the Prince that Lebedyev is again plotting against him. As Lebedyev himself confesses on the morning of the wedding, he has been trying without success to have the Prince declared insane. He even brought a doctor to visit Myshkin, but the physician was convinced of Myshkin's sanity.

Ippolit, who is extremely ill, continues to make sarcastic remarks at the expense of the Prince. Myshkin finally becomes quite angry and stops visiting him. However, the day before the wedding, Ippolit's mother begs the Prince to see her son who claims to have a secret to impart. When Myshkin finally arrives at Ippolit's bedside, the invalid merely warns him against Rogozhin. Pointing out that Rogozhin is abnormally passionate, Ippolit expresses the opinion that Rogozbin is capable of killing Aglaia to revenge himself on the Prince for taking Nastasya away from him.

Comment: Dostoyevsky indicates that Ippolit may be uttering these dire thoughts with the chief object of frightening Myshkin. This is of course what happens. However, Ippolit is right in warning the Prince about the lengths to which Rogozhin's passion may carry him. Although Ippolit's prediction does not come true, something equally tragic eventually occurs.

Nastasya has been trying, quite conscientiously, to cheer Myshkin up; her behavior seems so normal that he feels her symptoms of mental illness may be subsiding. He is particularly encouraged because she no longer seems to feel that she will ruin him by marrying him. At times, however, her symptoms recur. At one point, she becomes violently agitated, screaming that Rogozhin is in the garden and will kill her. Myshkin later learns that Rogozhin was in St. Petersburg while Nastasya was having this vision.

The night before the wedding, Nastasya again becomes extremely upset; but the following morning, Myshkin learns that she is quite happy and excited. The wedding is to occur in the evening. There is a large crowd waiting to see the bride leave for the church. Although they came with the intention of jeering, they are tremendously impressed with Nastasya's beauty. Just as she is about to enter the carriage, she sees Rogozhin in the crowd. Running up to him, Nastasya begs him to take her away. They get into the carriage and before anyone can stop them, Rogozhin directs the driver to take them to the train station.

Prince Myshkin expresses some surprise at what has happened, but adds that in Nastasya's condition, something of this sort might have been expected. Myshkin returns home, followed by a great many noisy people. Finally he invites them to come in, but only a few accept his invitation. He talks with them quietly and politely and they go home with a favorable impression of him. Afterward, Keller remarks to Lebedyev that while he would have started a fight, the Prince has made friends with his would-be persecutors.

Finally Myshkin is left alone. He tells Vera Lebedyev that he is going to St. Petersburg in the morning, but asks her to mention this to no one.

Comment: In this chapter we learn the following:

1) **General Ivolgin dies.**

2) **Nastasya, after urging that the wedding take place as soon as possible, sees Rogozhin and runs away with him, still dressed in her wedding gown.**

3) **Myshkin plans to follow Rogozhin and Nastasya to St. Petersburg.**

PART IV, CHAPTER 11

Myshkin arrives in St. Petersburg and immediately goes to Rogozhin's house. He is told that Rogozhin is not home, but as he leaves, he briefly sees Rogozhin looking at him from the window. Next he goes to the home of a widow with whom Nastasya stayed a few weeks before, but no one there has seen her. Showing great concern, the ladies of the family advise Myshkin to go back to Rogozhin's and if he still is not at home, to visit a friend of Nastasya's. Myshkin again finds no one at Rogozhin's home, but a porter tells him that Rogozhin spent the night at home but left early in the morning.

Nastasya's friend also has no news of her and, having quarreled with her, does not care what has become of her. Myshkin registers at the hotel where Rogozhin once tried to kill him and then, after going back to Rogozhin's house once more, returns to the widow's home. He acts very strangely there and asks to see the rooms which Nastasya occupied. He absent-mindedly puts a book he sees there in his pocket.

Returning to his hotel, Myshkin is filled with dread. Finally it occurs to him that Rogozhin will look for him if he is in trouble. However, the thought that he should remain where he is so that Rogozhin can find him does not prevent the Prince from restlessly going outside again. A short distance from the hotel, Rogozhin comes up and asks the Prince to come with him. Myshkin tells Rogozhin that he expected to see him in the hotel corridor. Rogozhin replies that he has been there.

Comment: Myshkin is referring to the stairway in which Rogozhin attempted to stab him (Part II, Chapter 5). It takes Myshkin several minutes to realize the significance of Rogozhin's reply that he was in the hotel corridor. Dostoyevsky does not elaborate on the reasons for Myshkin's sudden concern, but we can surmise that Rogozhin contemplated killing Myshkin.

Rogozhin says that they are going to his house but that they must walk on opposite sides of the street. Myshkin realizes that Rogozhin is afraid that someone will pass by, and wonders why he does not name the person he is looking for.

Comment: It is possible that Rogozhin fears that even now Nastasya, who is already dead, will escape him. He is afraid that someone will discover her body and take it away.

Finally they arrive at Rogozhin's house. Rogozhin motions the Prince to a chair and suggests that they spend the night together. However, Myshkin persists in asking about Nastasya. A curtain divides the study into two parts. Finally Rogozhin tells Myshkin that Nastasya is behind the curtain. Nastasya is lying on a bed, covered over completely by a white sheet. She is obviously dead. A fly's buzzing startles Myshkin.

Comment: The buzzing of the fly recalls Ippolit's image of the fly which has its place in the sun (Part III, Chapter 7). This reminds Myshkin that he has failed to help Nastasya, and by so failing, has lost his only chance to have a place in the world. The buzzing is the only sound in the room and presents an eerie contrast between life and death. Nastasya, who was so full of life, so talkative and noisy, is now dead.

Rogozhin admits that he killed Nastasya. Observing that Myshkin is trembling, he cautions him not to have an epileptic attack because this would attract people to the house. Rogozhin is afraid "they" will take Nastasya away.

Comment: Rogozhin has killed Nastasya because he feels that is the only way he can possess her. However, he is still afraid that he will not be able to keep her.

Myshkin agrees to stay with Rogozhin for the night, and the latter makes up a bed on the floor. Rogozhin explains that he has put disinfectant around the body and wonders whether they should buy flowers. Then he adds that this would only make them sad. He tells Myshkin that he used his "garden" knife to kill Nastasya, but does not know whether he planned to kill her when he took her from Pavlovsk.

Comment: The knife which Rogozhin used is the one which Myshkin observed several weeks before (Part II, Chapter 3) and the one with which Rogozhin tried to kill Myshkin. Flowers, of course, would emphasize the fact that Nastasya is dead. Although he has killed her, Rogozhin does not seem to grasp the idea that Nastasya is really dead.

After a while, Myshkin asks Rogozhin for the playing cards he used to entertain Nastasya.

Comment: Myshkin seems to be collecting mementoes to remind him of Nastasya.

Rogozhin suddenly laughs loudly, remembering the scene at the bandstand at Pavlovsk, when Nastasya struck the officer. Throughout the remainder of the night, Rogozhin is alternately quiet or loudly incoherent. The next morning, when they are discovered, Rogozhin is delirious and Myshkin, completely unaware of his surroundings, seems to be trying to soothe him.

Comment: Myshkin has reverted to his "idiotic" state. Dostoyevsky's description of Myshkin's attempts at comforting Rogozhin remind us of the way in which he tried to calm Nastasya (Part IV, Chapter 8). In both instances, Myshkin acts as though he were trying to comfort a child.

The final scene in the death chamber, although the climax of the novel, lacks the excessive emotion usually associated with such settings. In a way, it is anti-climactic, for the ending has long been foreseen. As a contrast to the previous high points of the novel, all of which have been accompanied by much noise and activity, the silence of this last scene is broken only by the buzzing of a fly and the maniacal laughter of Rogozhin.

PART IV, CHAPTER 12 CONCLUSION

Comment: In this final chapter, Dostoyevsky tries to "tie up the loose ends" of his novel.

The widow, to whom Myshkin had communicated his fear for Nastasya, goes to see Darya Alexeyevna in Pavlovsk. The two of them inform Lebedyev of their anxiety and he accompanies them to St. Petersburg. The three of them, with the police and Rogozhin's elder brother, break into Rogozhin's apartment the next morning. Rogozhin has brain fever, so his trial is delayed until his recovery. At his trial he gives a detailed account of the murder. His lawyer maintains that Rogozhin was not in his right mind when he committed the crime, and for this reason he is sentenced to "only" fifteen years at hard labor.

Comment: Rogozhin's sentence sounds severe, but in view of the harshness of the law at this period, it is really quite lenient. Murderers were almost always executed.

Dostoyevsky tells us that Ippolit finally died two weeks after Nastasya's murder, much to his own surprise. Most of the other characters in the novel continue living much as they did before the events Dostoyevsky has related. Radomsky has proved a true friend to Myshkin; through his efforts, the Prince was returned to Dr. Schneider's clinic in Switzerland, and Radomsky visits him frequently. Dr. Schneider is not hopeful about Myshkin's recovery. Radomsky occasionally sends news of Myshkin to Kolya and is also in communication with Vera Lebedyev. Dostoyevsky hints that they may marry.

Radomsky is also the source of information about the Epanchins. Aglaia suddenly marries a Polish "count" who, it turns out, is not a count, but a penniless adventurer. She has become a Roman Catholic and has broken off all communications with her family. Prince S. and Adelaida, after so many delays, have finally married. The entire Epanchin family (except for Aglaia) visited Myshkin in Switzerland and were quite distressed at his misfortune.

Dostoyevsky concludes the novel with Madame Epanchin's bitter protest against Europe where, as she says, they cannot even bake bread properly. She declares that Europe, and the Epanchins in Europe, are only fantasy.

Comment: Madame Epanchin here expresses Dostoyevsky's own feelings about Europe, and especially his belief that Russians belong in Russia and can only be happy there.

Comment(additional): The final chapter tells us what happened to various characters in the novel.

1) Rogozhin is sentenced to fifteen years in prison.

2) Myshkin is returned to Switzerland, but the chances of his recovery from mental illness are poor.

3) Ippolit dies.

4) Aglaia marries a bogus Polish count and becomes a Roman Catholic.

5) Radomsky goes to live abroad, shows great concern about Myshkin, and may eventually marry Vera Lebedyev.

6) Adelaida and Prince S. finally marry.

7) The Epanchins go abroad at last but are unhappy there.

THE IDIOT

. . . .

PRINCE MYSHKIN

Prince Myshkin is, of course, the central character of the book. We see and understand all the other participants as they react to and with him. Dostoyevsky's diaries and letters he wrote to friends while working on *The Idiot* leave no doubt that he consciously conceived of Myshkin as a Christ-like figure. The Prince has spent a number of years in Switzerland, high up in the mountains; there are overtones of Heaven in his description. The stories he tells us of his life there, his pity for the fallen and unfortunate, and his love for children (demonstrated by his warm relationship with young Kolya Ivolgin, who is practically a disciple) all remind us of passages in the New Testament. Although his appearance is also Christ-like, Dostoyevsky does not attempt to make Myshkin like Christ in every detail. This would be heresy of a sort, for Myshkin fails in his self-appointed mission, and the novelist is far too good a Christian to attribute this kind of failure to Christ. There is also the problem of the Prince's "idiocy." Myshkin's naivete, his ignorance of the most ordinary deceptions practiced by "civilized" people, are quite enough to have him branded as an "idiot." When people find out that these surface traits are only minor manifestations of his real character, composed of true humility and love for all his fellow men, it is no wonder that they consider him very odd indeed. In addition, Myshkin really is an epileptic. Yet in spite of all these disabilities, everyone with whom the Prince comes in contact is strangely affected and impressed by him. They find themselves telling him their most intimate thoughts, and asking his advice when they hardly know him. The Epanchin girls seem to take his measure immediately, and we can guess that Aglaia's love for the Prince dates from this first meeting. Although he has not been invited, Nastasya greets him at her birthday party as an old friend. During the course of the evening she not only asks his advice about her marriage, but says she will abide by his decision.

THE PRINCE AS AN ACTIVE FORCE

Because the Prince's role in *The Idiot* is essentially a passive one, we should not assume that he does not exert an active influence on the other characters. For one thing, he is a shrewd judge of character and the motives of others, and he is liable to state his opinions with devastating honesty. These traits anger the weak Gavril Ivolgin (Ganya); the young man who cannot decide whether to marry Nastasya or Aglaia is infuriated that anyone else should have such a clear idea of his vacillation and lack of purpose. Others besides Ganya find contact with the Prince disturbing, despite the fascination he exerts upon them. The emotions which Lebedyev and Ippolit express towards Myshkin have as much of hate as of love in them. They seem to feel that his honesty, in some unspoken way, is forcing them towards actions they do not want to take. In these relationships, as in others in the novel, the Prince acts upon others through the force of his personality rather than by direct action or speech.

MYSHKIN'S "MISSION"

When he does try to influence people directly, the Prince almost invariably fails. His "mission," to bring about a Russian moral renaissance through a re-emphasis on the virtues of humility and love for one's fellow men (his own virtues), meets determined resistance. When people hear him expound his ideas, the usual reaction is to call him an "idiot." Even the members of his own class, the representatives of the hereditary nobility who are gathered at the Epanchin's party at Pavlovsk, smile and say that his ideas are "not practical." The only ones who really understand him (except for Aglaia and Nastasya, whose emotional involvement makes it impossible for them to be objective) are Kolya Ivolgin, who is still a child, and the delightful Madame Epanchin, who cheerfully admits that in many ways she will always be childish. As the other characters in the novel find, the genuinely simple character cannot be understood by those who have neither simplicity nor honesty.

THE PRINCE'S EFFECT ON OTHERS

Although the Prince is completely honest and has the best possible intentions, contact with him ends in disaster for a number of people. The reason for his unfortunate effect, and Dostoyevsky's intention when he resolves the story in this way, are among the most difficult questions to answer about *The Idiot*. It seems unlikely that Dostoyevsky is trying to say that Christ was unsuccessful in his mission of attaining redemption for all men, though the author is certainly aware that the modern world is unchristian in many ways. Part of the difficulty can be attributed to the dramatic nature of the novel; sometimes the author puts several characters together and then seems to sit back and watch them interact, serving as the recorder rather than the inventor of his scenes. While this kind of explanation can be carried to ridiculous lengths, there are inconsistencies and unclear places in the novel which can best be explained in these dramatic terms. For example, why should Myshkin, who has already stated twice that his illness makes it impossible for him to marry, seriously contemplate marriage first with Aglaia and then with Nastasya, in Part IV of *The Idiot*? We can only assume the Prince is caught up in the dramatic situation and forgets his disability. Perhaps the best inclusive explanation for the Prince's failure is his inability to interact with people on a human level. He is full of love, even a sort of personification of it, but it is a God-like love which the other characters cannot understand or are unprepared to accept. Rogozhin, who sees himself in the Prince, has a peculiar love for him that is mixed with hatred. Aglaia, though she understands him in part, is perturbed because he has a Don Quixote-like character and does not behave like a real man. Ippolit, when he reads his "Essential Explanation," is looking for a strong reaction, for violent argument, not for the kind of gentle understanding which the Prince is able to give him. Even the scapegrace General Ivolgin finds the "idiot" an unsatisfactory audience for his incredible tall stories. He would rather be called a liar, as he usually is, than be "patronized" by Myshkin's acceptance. The Prince's greatest failure, of course, is with Nastasya. To simplify a complex situation, what Nastasya wants from Myshkin is human love. What she gets from him is a kind of super-human pity, and she finds this so intolerable that she turns from it to the death which she clearly foresees at Rogozhin's hands. To an only slightly less intense degree, Aglaia too unsuccessfully seeks a human relationship with the Prince, and she too turns from his inhuman love to ruin. (To Dostoyevsky, marriage with a fraudulent Polish count, a Roman Catholic and a "Westerner," is the most terrible end imaginable.)

MYSHKIN'S FAILURE

Thus for all the uncanny attraction that he exerts, Myshkin fails because people find themselves unable to accept the combination of brotherly love, pity, and understanding which he offers them. Dostoyevsky may be saying through the character of Myshkin that the world, or Russia in particular, has departed so widely from the Christian ideal, and is so occupied with its own materialistic concerns, that people can no longer react to the kind of love that Christ has to offer. Alternatively, he may be saying that a simply passive good is not sufficient in the modern world; an active principle is also necessary. Myshkin tries to inspire others by his example, but apparently example is not enough. It is even possible that the author feels that human love, in the last analysis, is preferable to the divine but necessarily distant love of God for his children on earth. The question of what Dostoyevsky intends to express in the character of Prince Myshkin is not one that can be given a single, definitive answer. Whatever the writer meant, the book itself tells us that those whom he tries hardest to help fare worst, and the Prince himself lapses into his former "idiocy" as the net result of his return to his homeland.

ROGOZHIN

Dostoyevsky intends Rogozhin to be Myshkin's double; that is, he means to show Rogozhin as essentially the same kind of man as the Prince, but one who uses the potential of his personality for evil as Myshkin uses his for good. In this the author is not entirely successful. He has no difficulty in portraying Rogozhin as an evil man (he is unmistakably the villain of the story), but the **clichés** which Dostoyevsky borrows from the contemporary horror tale appreciably diminish the effectiveness of the picture.

Rogozhin is not of the Prince's stature, he is not as well developed a character, nor is he as interesting. (Ordinarily, evil characters are much easier to depict, and are often more interesting than the good ones.) Rogozhin's vice is the obverse of Myshkin's virtue; it is lust instead of love. He is a man with a one-track mind, driven to any lengths by his desire for Nastasya. The Prince points out to him that this compelling desire is a part of his personality; if it did not have Nastasya as its object Rogozhin would have turned into a miser like his father. Dostoyevsky does not make very clear whether Rogozhin desires Nastasya sexually or whether he sees her primarily as a possession. The latter possibility seems more likely, for he thinks of the woman almost exclusively as an acquisition, in terms of how many rubles it will cost to "buy" her. This attitude makes the **climax** of the story logical, for the only way in which Rogozhin can possess Nastasya completely is to kill her. Rogozhin is aware of the bond between Prince Myshkin and himself. He wants to exchange crosses with Myshkin in the hope that the Prince's cross will act as a talisman to ward off the crime he knows to be imminent. Ironically, this effort is in vain, for the evil is within himself. Rogozhin, like the demonic heroes of Dostoyevsky's other novels, surrenders meekly once the crime has been committed, does not attempt to defend his action, and accepts his punishment as just. The murder has been a kind of catharsis for him, a moral turning point, and though the author does not say so, we assume that the rest of his life will be an atonement for the deed.

NASTASYA

The character of Nastasya in *The Idiot* is based in part on Dostoyevsky's fiery mistress, Polina Suslova, and also in part on Martha Brown, a rather pathetic woman who seems to have traveled through most of Europe under the "protection" of one

man after another, and who finally came to rest in Russia, where
Dostoyevsky met her. Nastasya is a rather brilliant portrayal of
the woman wronged, who looks in ever more anguished ways
for relief from her feelings of guilt and her unattainable desire
for respectability. She was seduced when hardly more than a
child by the hardened "connoisseur" of women, Afanasy Totsky.
Even at this early age, she is a person of strong character, and
her first shock quickly turns to contempt for her seducer. When
she hears that Totsky is about to contract a respectable marriage
she follows him to St. Petersburg and effectively calls a halt to
his plans. Totsky fears her self-reliant nature, her intelligence,
and her satirical wit, and tries to marry her off to Ganya so that
he can go ahead with his own marriage. Nastasya is faced with
three choices in marriage, all of them impossible. Ganya, though
he is impressed by her beauty, is primarily concerned with the
money he will get from Totsky for marrying her. A union with
Rogozhin, Nastasya can see, will only end fatally for herself
because of his maniacally possessive nature. And she herself
will not accept marriage with Prince Myshkin, though he asks
her several times. She sees his love, correctly, as a kind of pity,
though she underestimates the depth of that pity. Her guilt over
her "immoral" life (which Dostoyevsky takes pains to point out
is no fault of hers) turns into an inverted pride, and she flaunts
her outrageous behavior before the respectable citizens of
Pavlovsk. Her inability to find any way out of her plight is fuel
for her already highly excitable nature, until we begin to see the
signs of madness in her which Myshkin is the first to detect. The
confrontation with Aglaia, whom Nastasya views as a haughty
and self-righteous aristocrat, serves as a trigger to release her
pent-up anger and aggression. She easily wins Myshkin away
from the more normal (and thus less pitiable) Aglaia, but
abandons the Prince at the church door. Her headlong flight
with Rogozhin is deliberately suicidal; she feels that the only
solution to her problems is death. Myshkin, Madame Epanchin,

and Adelaida are all correct when, looking at her portrait, they see beauty, power and suffering in her face.

AGLAIA EPANCHIN

Aglaia completes the quartet of major characters in *The Idiot*. Some of her traits are based on those of Anna Korvin-Krukovskaya, a flighty, artistic girl of twenty who sent stories to a periodical published by Dostoyevsky. Dostoyevsky became interested, visited her, and promptly fell in love. Though somewhat scatter-brained, Anna had sense enough to refuse a proposal of marriage from the middle-aged writer with a history of epilepsy and no prospects. Aglaia is by far the most normal of the four major figures, and one of the most attractive women in Dostoyevsky's novels. She is sensitive, proud, high-spirited and quick-tempered, and bored with her rather stupid middle-class family. Prince Myshkin attracts her as soon as he appears because he is so utterly unlike all the other people she meets in her day-to-day existence. While it is with Aglaia that Prince Myshkin's relationship comes closest to ordinary, human love, it is in relation to her that we see how he is really incapable of this kind of love. In spite of repeated evidence, she is unable to believe that pity provides a far stronger motivation for the Prince than sexual attraction. Finally, she makes the tactical error of arranging a face-to-face confrontation with the more clever, more experienced and stronger-willed Nastasya. Nastasya has almost decided to give the Prince up, but Aglaia challenges her pride. She understands Myshkin's character far more clearly than the young Aglaia does, and with a true instinct arranges the scene so that the Prince must choose between his love for Aglaia and his pity for the older woman. The choice is a foregone conclusion; the Prince, almost without hesitation, chooses Nastasya. Aglaia's flight from Russia is an imitation, on a smaller scale in keeping with her less developed character, of Nastasya's flight to death. She admires the bogus Polish count she marries for his "nobility of soul"; it is obvious that she is looking for a second Myshkin. It is curious that we are very much affected by Aglaia's "little" tragedy. Perhaps it is because in this crowd of tension-ridden, suffering people we turn to her relative normality as a reviving change. Her intellectual airs, her dizzying changes of mood, her transparent pretenses, her very youth, endear her to us. It is because we see in her such a potential for happiness that her misfortune affects us so deeply. We can rationalize to ourselves that the other major characters were doomed whether or not the Prince appeared on the scene, but if he is guilty of anything, he is guilty of Aglaia's unhappiness.

IPPOLIT

Ippolit Terentyev does not play a large part in the action of *The Idiot*; he is one of Dostoyevsky's "digressions." Yet we have the feeling that Ippolit is making, in his involved and turgid way, a commentary on the action of the story. He is one of Dostoyevsky's "underground men," solitary, introspective, and in his own case, in the final stages of tuberculosis. At the beginning he is presented as one of the nihilists; in depicting them Dostoyevsky is trying to show the immaturity and basic selfishness of their revolutionary ideas. But during the scenes in Pavlovsk, Ippolit becomes considerably more than this, and we can see the author's attitude toward him becoming more sympathetic. He is a type, familiar from Dostoyevsky's other novels, who is always striving with inadequate physical or mental equipment to achieve great things. In Ippolit's case the tension is increased by the fact that he knows he has only a few weeks to live. He feels that he has a message to give the world, but his "Essential Explanation" is vague and almost totally formless, and he realizes that he has not expressed what he feels obscurely within him. Part of the author's purpose in this portrait is to show the futility of intellectual strivings which have atheism as their foundation and thus leave God out of the account, though Ippolit seems to be trying at the same time to fashion his own definition of God. This effort is difficult for him because he sees only the malevolent forces in the world, in contrast to Myshkin who looks at the possible beauty in life. In his feverish and hypersensitive state, in part the result of his tuberculosis, Ippolit is aware of forces and relationships which are hidden from others. His dream of the spider is a vision of the evil forces in the world, and his connection of Rogozhin with these forces is accurate. In the same way he is aware of Prince Myshkin's essential goodness, and in his twisted mind, hates him for being able to be so optimistic. He is also aware, as very few of the other characters are, that Myshkin and Rogozhin are complementary characters, each dependent on the other. Dostoyevsky's offhand dismissal of his death is rather disappointing. We expect an agonized deathbed scene, but perhaps this idea was too melodramatic even for Dostoyevsky.

GAVRIL IVOLGIN (GANYA)

Ganya is one of Dostoyevsky's striving, expectant people who do not have the intelligence, the drive or the will to succeed. He is part of the submerged class whose fortunes are far lower than their social position. He resents his poverty so bitterly that he is willing to do absolutely anything to gain wealth and status. Because of his weak nature, his inability to follow one unvarying course of action, he continually fails. The author has sketched his character so skillfully that we feel only contempt for Ganya. We first see him when he is involved in negotiations to marry Nastasya, Totsky's ex-mistress; to offset the blow to his pride in marrying a kept woman there is the sum of 75,000 rubles. Yet in addition to the financial compensation, Ganya admits that he intends to "punish" the beautiful Nastasya after they are married. The **irony** of Ganya's statement that he will bring into submission the proud Nastasya, whose will and intelligence are so much more powerful than his own, is obvious to the reader but not to Ganya. Dostoyevsky makes the young man's lack of character devastatingly apparent during Nastasya's birthday party. Nastasya offers him the bundle of money if he will pull it out of the fire, and Ganya faints because he cannot resolve the struggle between his pride and his greed. He asks Aglaia to "save" him from an unworthy marriage with Nastasya, and meets with the contempt he deserves. Ganya is one of the few people in the story who actually hates Prince Myshkin. He rages at the fact that both Aglaia and Nastasya love the Prince, and his small mind envies Myshkin's open-heartedness and generosity. At the beginning of Part IV, Dostoyevsky inserts a long discussion on the difficulty of writing about the perfectly ordinary, "commonplace" character. Ganya is just such a figure, as the author points out. Dramatically, his purpose is to provide contrast; unlike all the overwrought people in the book with one-track minds, Ganya has a no-track mind.

THE EPANCHIN FAMILY

As a member of the principal quartet of characters, Aglaia has been discussed already. The rest of the Epanchins can be treated as a group because part of their importance lies in the fact that they are a family. Dostoyevsky likes to discuss people as members of family groups; the "family" personality is established first, and then individual members are shown as variations of the pattern. The Epanchins are stalwart members of the Russian upper middle class which was composed of Army officers and civil servants. Although Madame Epanchin is the former Princess Myshkin, the family pretension to higher social status is largely unsuccessful. Aglaia, and perhaps her sisters as well, find the atmosphere at home boring and her family's friends tedious. The character of General Epanchin, as Dostoyevsky presents it to us, is somewhat contradictory. We see him at the beginning of the novel scheming to marry off Nastasya to his secretary Ganya Ivolgin, so that the General can make her his mistress. His behavior during his first interview with Prince Myshkin is both stupid and patronizing. Later in the book, however, he appears as the good-hearted and doting though none-too-bright father who attempts to comfort Aglaia. Madame Epanchin is a more important and more interesting character. Her relationship with Prince Myshkin is not merely one of blood; she has a good deal of his direct, honest approach to things. In many ways they are both, as she cheerfully admits, children who have never grown up. Like a child, however, she has retained a shrewd insight into character; her judgments, though they usually sound silly at the time, are the true ones. For the rest, she is a fussy, slightly rattlebrained mother, brooding over her daughters like a hen over her chicks. She admits frankly that she finds their behavior incomprehensible, but loves them no less for all that. In *The Idiot's* world of rapacious adults, Madame Epanchin's intelligent and unselfish childishness is refreshingly normal. Aglaia's two sisters, Alexandra and Adelaida, serve largely as a foil for Aglaia herself. Though they show flashes of her wit and intuition, their correct social deportment as marriageable young ladies of good family contrasts sharply with Aglaia's wildly erratic behavior.

THE IVOLGIN FAMILY

Old General Ivolgin, the father of the family, is a pathological liar and a drunkard, but like Falstaff in Shakespeare's *Henry IV*, there is very little harm in him. He retains his pride from the days of his prosperity, and is deeply offended when his audience points out the impossible nature of his incredibly tall tales. Ippolit's mother, Marfa Terentyev, is his mistress, but she lends him money rather than the other way around. His utterly unbelievable story that he was Napoleon's page and personally suggested the retreat from Moscow is the **climax** of his inventive powers. It is typical of the old man's pride that he should take Myshkin's polite acceptance of this story as some kind of veiled insult. Varvara (Varya) and Kolya Ivolgin, the children of the General and his long-suffering wife Nina Alexandrovna, are two of the warmest and most human characters in the story. Varya is the epitome of the dutiful daughter and sister; we feel that she marries Ptitsyn largely to provide a home for her family, and she even tries to plead the case of her unpleasant brother Ganya with Aglaia Epanchin. Kolya is still an adolescent, and Dostoyevsky achieves in him a charming and highly successful portrait of a child, which is a difficult literary feat. Kolya does not understand most of the wiles of the adult world around him, and he saddles himself with the care of a drunken father, but he remains cheerful and willing. His relationship with Myshkin is probably supposed to be that of master and disciple, and his naive admiration for the Prince is very clear. Nevertheless, his mind is too healthy to devote his life to a lost cause; the author's remark that Kolya will probably become a useful member of society comments directly on Myshkin's good influence and ironically on the Prince's own failure. The honesty and cheerfulness of Varya and Kolya are intended to contrast with the scheming and ill temper of their brother Ganya.

LUKYAN AND VERA LEBEDYEV

Lukyan Lebedyev and his daughter Vera are intended to present as strong a contrast as the Ivolgin children. Lebedyev himself is one of Dostoyevsky's "underground men." He is cunning and unsociable, eager to take advantage of those weaker than himself, and servile to those whose wealth or social position put them above him. To Dostoyevsky he represents, on a petty scale, the evil which Rogozhin symbolizes in its full flowering. Lebedyev does not do very much harm, but he does as much as he can. His character is demonstrated by his continual betrayal of Prince Myshkin, which culminates in his attempt to have the Prince declared insane on the morning of his wedding to Nastasya. His cruelty is particularly apparent in his tormenting of General Ivolgin after the drunken General has stolen some money from him. Although Ivolgin stealthily returns the money, the sadistic Lebedyev persists in ignoring it, and the General eventually becomes so upset that he suffers a stroke. The fact that Lebedyev enjoys humiliating himself as much as others (witness his frequent "confessions" to Myshkin), and his statement that he has never loved General Ivolgin better than when he is torturing him, are further evidence of his perverted personality. Vera Lebedyev is as different from her father as it is possible to be. Just as Lebedyev plays Judas to Myshkin's Christ, so Vera plays the part of Martha in the New Testament, who self-effacingly waited on Jesus. Part of Myshkin's insensitivity to human love is that he never realizes that Vera worships him. The reader feels that the note on Vera in the last chapter, which seems to predict her marriage to Radomsky, promises a just reward which has been long delayed.

RADOMSKY

We do not get to know Yevgeny Radomsky very well as we read *The Idiot*, and we feel that the cool, reserved intellectual wants it that way. Radomsky is a specimen of the completely Westernized Russian. He travels extensively in Europe and returns to find his native Russia as strange as Africa. At first he thinks that Myshkin's peculiar behavior is "typically Russian," but eventually he too falls under the Prince's spell to some degree. Radomsky is so detached that he can take the situation calmly even when his courtship of Aglaia founders because of Myshkin's presence. In fact, he even lectures the Prince on the necessity for natural, human love, and tells him that Myshkin's love for Nastasya, founded on pity, must end badly. Dostoyevsky may be trying to make the point that Radomsky's detachment is no more effective than Myshkin's over-involvement. Eventually, and ironically, Radomsky is affected by the Prince's concern for others; it is he who takes steps to have the insane "idiot" returned to the Swiss sanitarium.

FERDYSHTCHENKO

Ferdyshtchenko is so self-effacing that we never even learn his first name and patronymic. In perfect keeping with his need for self-abasement, it is Ferdyshtchenko who proposes the "parlor game" at Nastasya's birthday party, where each participant is to tell the worst action of his life, and his own story is just the mean, petty deed we expect to hear. Dostoyevsky admired the writing of Charles Dickens, the English novelist; the character of Ferdyshtchenko, and parts of Lebedyev's character, are consciously modeled on that of the obsequious Mr. Micawber in Dickens' David Copperfield.

THE NIHILISTS

Except for Ippolit, who plays a much more important role, the young radicals who attack Prince Myshkin in Pavlovsk are not individualized very much by Dostoyevsky. In his hatred for their political principles, the author makes them simply stupid and malevolent. He wishes to prove that all the socialist and atheist talk about freedom is simply a mask for personal selfishness and greed; any doctrine which tries to leave God out of the account is doomed before it starts. Antip Burdovsky, who pretends to be the illegitimate son of Myshkin's benefactor Pavlishtchev, is the weak-minded pawn of those cleverer than he is. Vladimir Doktorenko, Lebedyev's nephew, is a malicious adventurer. The only member of the gang with any redeeming features is the oafish Keller, who tends to think with his fists but is capable of kind impulses in his dim-witted way. It is interesting to see that Keller rather quickly comes over to Prince Myshkin's side. The Prince is capable of converting stupidity, but not the malice of the other nihilists.

THE IDIOT

CRITICAL COMMENTARY

. . . .

INTRODUCTION

The prime difficulty in trying to deal analytically with any successful work of art, and critics agree that *The Idiot* is such a work, is that the whole is greater in its effect upon us than the sum of all the parts into which we can divide it. *The Idiot* is at the same time a coherent story; a remarkable portrait gallery of characters; an outlet for and product of Dostoyevsky's own ideas on religion, politics and social and psychological questions; an attempt at prophecy; and a vehicle for disguised material from Dostoyevsky's own life. Yet when we have finished reading the book we feel the emotional impact which is the attribute of a truly great novel; it is the work as a whole which impresses us. Nevertheless, analysis of the components of *The Idiot* is necessary; it can give us an intellectual as well as emotional appreciation of the work. *The Idiot* can be examined most effectively by treating it as a novel in which ideas provide the motivation for construction of the story in a particular way. Then we can attempt to see how the individual characters and the interactions between them illustrate the ideas in which the author is interested. The Character Analyses section also approaches the book from this point of view.

SOURCES

Like all great authors, Dostoyevsky digests his sources thoroughly, and their influence is not always easy to trace. In *The Idiot* we find evidence of the Russian author's early interest in the French Romantic writers, in the German author Hoffmann (the author of the fantasies called the *Tales of Hofmann*), and in contemporary tales of mystery and horror. These influences account for the mysterious tone of parts of *The Idiot*, in particular Prince Myshkin's visit to Rogozhin's home in St. Petersburg, the final macabre "wake" over Nastasya's body, and details such as Rogozhin's "burning eyes" (the eyes of the magician in the conventional horror tale) and the weird components of Ippolit's dreams. Much of *The Idiot* has the melodramatic tone of Romantic fiction. Other important influences were those of the French author Balzac and Dostoyevsky's immediate predecessor in Russia, Nikolai Gogol. The realistic novels of these two writers provide much of the inspiration for Dostoyevsky's early work and help to account for his concentration on the life of the lower and middle classes. Dostoyevsky, himself a product of the middle class, is never comfortable when depicting the nobility, and the portraits of the aristocrats at the Epanchins' "engagement party" for Aglaia and Myshkin are cleverly satirical but somewhat unconvincing. In the great division between Realistic and Romantic novels, Dostoyevsky is firmly on the Romantic side. The Realists try to provide such a profusion of accurate details and authenticity of atmosphere that the reader feels that he is reading a "slice of life." The Romantic novelist, on the other hand, builds his own world within the novel and entices the reader into that world so skillfully that he goes on believing in what he reads no matter how fantastic the novel-world becomes. Dostoyevsky is a Romantic novelist; the stage on which *The Idiot* is enacted is nothing like the world we know, but we believe in it.

SOURCES FOR THE THEME OF THE NOVEL

For the **theme** of the novel the real sources are the New Testament, and *Don Quixote* by the Spanish Renaissance writer Cervantes. The character of Myshkin, as has been noted earlier, is modeled on Christ. Evidently Dostoyevsky did not intend to represent Christ exactly nor to make a precise parallel between Christ's earthly ministry and Myshkin's career in Russia, but he did intend Myshkin to remind the reader of Christ at every turn. Dostoyevsky also had in mind the career of Cervantes' knight, who lived to the fullest extent according to the already outdated code of chivalry, behaving in the manner which we still call "quixotic." Yet another source is the character of Iago in Shakespeare's play *Othello*.

THEME OF THE NOVEL

The **theme** of *The Idiot*, if it can be compressed into a sentence, is that the passively good man cannot survive when confronted with the active evil of the modern world. Prince Myshkin is a good influence on nearly all those with whom he comes in contact, but the lives of all the important characters, Nastasya, Aglaia and Rogozhin, end in disaster because the Prince cannot act.

PRINCE MYSHKIN'S "MISSION"

Myshkin's "mission" is to save the Russian people from materialism, atheism and the preachings of the advocates of socialism and "enlightened self-interest." There are obvious parallels with Christ's ministry on earth. The Prince is either diverted from his mission by his meeting with Nastasya and Rogozhin, or else this encounter is his first trial; Dostoyevsky's intention here is unclear. We see the **theme** of the mission reappearing as Myshkin talks with those of his own rank at the Epanchins' "engagement party," but this attempt to spread his doctrine culminates in an epileptic seizure. At the end of the novel Myshkin's self-appointed task seems entirely lost in his personal entanglements. It is possible that the author intends this ending to represent a kind of ultimate salvation brought about by the Prince. In death, Nastasya finds a peace she could not have achieved in life, and Rogozhin's calm acceptance of his punishment may be meant to indicate the beginning of his redemption.

THE THEME OF THE "DOUBLE"

A type of character which particularly fascinated the writer, and which we find occurring in several of his novels (particularly *The Double* and *Crime and Punishment*), is the double or split personality. This kind of character has a tremendous potential for either good or evil. The usual pattern of Dostoyevsky's novels is for this "double" character to commit a terrible crime and then to realize the evil he has done and try to atone for his sin. Dostoyevsky first conceived of the "idiot" as this kind of double character with almost infinite capacities for good and evil. At one point he said that the "idiot" would be based upon the character of Iago, the truly terrible villain of Shakespeare's play *Othello*, but that the Russian character would end divinely. In this, the novelist set himself so difficult a task that he began seven different versions of the novel before the final one. Finally Dostoyevsky decided to split his "double" character into two separate figures, with the good side becoming the "idiot" Prince

Myshkin and the evil side Rogozhin. This proved a much more workable plan.

STRUCTURE OF THE NOVEL

The most obvious divisions of *The Idiot* are those imposed by time. The first part of the novel is set in St. Petersburg, and all the events occur within the same day. (Dostoyevsky, incidentally, wrote this long section of the book in just twenty-three days.) The second part opens six months after the first, just after Myshkin's return to St. Petersburg from Moscow. The action in this portion begins in St. Petersburg but the scene soon changes to the summer resort of Pavlovsk. The events cover approximately two weeks and end with the climactic confrontation between Aglaia and Nastasya. (This division of *The Idiot* occupies Parts II, III, and the first eight chapters of Part IV.) Another interval of nearly three weeks is occupied by Nastasya's preparations for her wedding with Prince Myshkin, and ends with her precipitous flight to St. Petersburg with Rogozhin (Part IV, Chapters 9 and 10). The final scenes of *The Idiot* begin in St. Petersburg on the morning after Nastasya's escape and end with the weird vigil of the Prince and Rogozhin during the ensuing night. Dostoyevsky utilizes a final chapter of four pages to tie up all the loose ends of his narrative. From this point of view the novel is episodic, that is, has short **episodes** of violent action crowded into a few hours alternating with periods of weeks or months during which very little happens. The circumstances under which he wrote (*The Idiot* was published serially) had a great effect on the structure of the novel. Dostoyevsky had to maintain the reader's interest over a period of months. This accounts in part for the dramatic chapter endings.

THE IDIOT AS A DRAMATIC WORK

Although *The Idiot* is episodic, a number of critics have pointed
out that this flaw is more apparent than real. We do not notice
any inconsistencies of time when reading the novel, because
Dostoyevsky's method is essentially dramatic. *The Idiot* is
written with many of the techniques that would be used in
writing a play. In contrast, the Russian novelist Tolstoy used
the **epic** style (the technique of the long, sweeping narrative)
for *War and Peace* and *Anna Karenina*. From this dramatic point
of view, *The Idiot* contains several great "scenes" which mark
high points in the action. These scenes usually indicate crises in
the plot and turning points in the lives of the major characters.
The passages between these scenes are usually at a much lower
level of tension and serve as transitional material.

DRAMATIC "SCENES" IN THE IDIOT

The first of these important episodes is Myshkin's initial
encounter with the Epanchin family. The Prince's long
monologue here serves to make his character and his position
as a Christ-figure absolutely clear, while Aglaia's remarks reveal
her interest in him and look forward to the relationship between
the two later in the story. The second high point, more important
still, is marked by the frenzied action at Nastasya's birthday
party. There is a series of melodramatic incidents, for instance
Nastasya's derisive act in challenging Ganya to pull a bundle of
ruble notes out of the fire. In this scene we get our clearest look
so far at the characters of Ferdyshtchenko, Totsky and General
Epanchin, and begin to understand Nastasya's feverishly active,
guilt-ridden personality. We also see the strange power which
the Prince's innocence and goodness wield over people who
are almost strangers to him. The closing part of the scene, in

which Ptitsyn and Totsky stroll home in the snow, discussing the events of the evening, is very like the epilogue of a play. The other important scenes in *The Idiot* include Myshkin's encounter with the Nihilists: Burdovsky, Keller, Doktorenko and Ippolit Terentyev; the Prince's birthday party at which he hints that he will abandon his mission and at which Ippolit reads his "Essential Explanation," a central **exposition** of Dostoyevsky's symbolism in the novel; and the Epanchins' "engagement party" for Aglaia and the Prince, at which Myshkin finally proves to himself and others that he is incapable of carrying out his "mission" to reform the Russians.

DRAMATIC CLIMAX

Dramatically speaking, the **climax** of *The Idiot* occurs with the confrontation between Aglaia and Nastasya. This tragic scene, in which the sensitive, proud aristocrat and the clever and equally emotional "fallen woman" quarrel over Myshkin, could be presented effectively, almost without change, on the stage. We can tell from the atmosphere of the episode that its sequel must be fatal. The final act of the play is an intentionally shocking contrast to the passionate excitement, the fervid activity and sense of movement which the other scenes generate. We have as finale the silent, desolate vigil of the Prince and Rogozhin over the dead body of Nastasya. In place of Nastasya's feverish talk, there is only the languid buzzing of a fly.

APPRAISAL OF THE IDIOT AS DRAMA

When looked at as a series of brilliant scenes, *The Idiot* is a highly artistic achievement. Dostoyevsky can handle crowds magnificently, so that we are continuously aware of each person in the room, of his relationship to every other person there, and of the effect each one is trying to produce on the others. An example of this technique at work can be seen in Ippolit's "Explanation," in which the dying youth alternately plays up to his audience and loses himself in his philosophy. The almost unbearable tension of these **episodes** is broken only to be built up and broken again. From the point of view of writing skill, the conception of the novel as this series of scenes and the development of the scenes themselves can be considered Dostoyevsky's greatest accomplishment in *The Idiot*.

FLAWS IN THE NOVEL

When regarded as an attempt at continuous narrative rather than as a dramatic work, the flaws in *The Idiot* become more apparent. The structure is somewhat rambling. There are so many subplots, and the relationships between the characters are so complex, that we sometimes lose sight of the larger issues and ideas. There are times when we feel that Dostoyevsky does not know, from one chapter to the next, how he is going to resolve the various conflicts. (We know from his letters that the ending surprised Dostoyevsky as much as it did his readers.) The number of characters seems to multiply as the book progresses. We should remember, of course, that Dostoyevsky is trying to give us a large view, almost a survey of Russian life, but even so the "cast of thousands" gets rather unwieldy. In the same way, a number of ideas are introduced only to be dropped or treated inconsistently. Ippolit's remarks about freedom and charity, for instance, seems to be suggested once and then abandoned. A more serious charge is that a few of the characters seem to behave inconsistently or develop in illogical ways. General Epanchin, for example, who initially appears as a rather unpleasant man who wants Nastasya as his mistress, is later depicted as a rather sympathetic, doting father. Much the same objection can be made to some of the symbols in *The Idiot*. For instance, we cannot be sure whether the symbolism of the fly is paradoxical intentionally or accidentally. There are times, too, when Dostoyevsky seems to forget that he has already told us something.

RELIGIOUS IDEAS IN THE IDIOT

Dostoyevsky's religious ideas are central to *The Idiot*. Myshkin is shown as Christ-like in the sense that he is a person of absolute humility and goodness, one who is ready to take the sins of the world upon himself. In the figure of Myshkin, Dostoyevsky is preaching the reign of Christian love, which within the formal framework of the Russian Orthodox Church and the Tsarist government of Russia, will bring about the spiritual renaissance that the Russians so desperately need. The writer goes even farther. He believes in the pan-Slavic theory of Russia as the "Third Rome," that is, of the Russians as a God-fearing people, like the Jews in ancient times, whose duty is to bring the enlightenment of the Orthodox faith to the other nations of Europe. These nations, according to Dostoyevsky, have been undermined by the evils of atheism, socialism and Roman Catholicism, for the Roman Church has been perverted by its hierarchy. Sin, to Dostoyevsky, is less a matter of deeds than of a state of mind; although Nastasya has technically been living in sin, he condemns her far less than he does Burdovsky and Doktorenko. Ineffectual though they are, they are pilloried because they have been trying to lead others astray with their nihilistic philosophy. The author's emphasis on the individual can be seen in the **theme**, recurrent in Dostoyevsky's novels, of salvation through suffering. Myshkin, as the Christ-like man, cannot suffer for his own sins as do Raskolnikov in *Crime and*

Punishment and Ivan Karamazov in *The Brothers Karamazov*; instead he suffers for the sins of others.

POLITICAL IDEAS

The political ideas in *The Idiot* are, in a sense, an outgrowth of Dostoyevsky's religious thought. After his youthful involvement with the radicals of the Petrashevsky Circle, followed by his trial and imprisonment, the writer became a staunch conservative. The scene in which Burdovsky, Ippolit and their friends try to extort money from the Prince with the tale that Burdovsky is his benefactor's illegitimate child, is intended to make the nihilists look ridiculous. Dostoyevsky attacks this revolutionary group on moral grounds. The unlimited freedom of the individual which the nihilists demand necessarily includes a lack of Christian love for one's neighbor and will end, he feels, in the slavery of the individual under socialism. Since, from an anti-Communist point of view, this is what happened after the Russian Revolution of 1917, it is no wonder that some of Dostoyevsky's admirers call him prophetic. The writer feels that socialist ideas are entering Russia from Europe. As a result, he opposes the intellectuals, such as the contemporary novelist Turgenyev, who want to "Westernize" Russia. Dostoyevsky favors reliance on the Russian spirit, in which he has an almost mystical belief. When aroused by the Christian love which Myshkin represents, the author feels that the Russian spirit will be capable of rejuvenating not only Russia, but of reviving the "dead" Europe as well.

THE "UNDERGROUND MAN"

A **theme** which appears in a number of Dostoyevsky's novels, and is important in *The Idiot*, is that of the "underground man."

This concept has its origin partly in the circumstances of the author's own life, and partly in his social ideas. The underground man is an isolated, lonely figure (like Dostoyevsky himself in his early life) who is sensitive, self-analytical and addicted to violent sensation. Dostoyevsky's compulsive gambling is an instance of this need for intense excitement. The idea of the underground man is central to several of Dostoyevsky's novels, such as *Notes from Underground* and *The Insulted and Injured*. The oppressed man, usually of the lower classes, is alternately the victim of others and their persecutor. In *The Idiot* we can see these ideas in the almost masochistic way in which Lebedyev and Ferdyshtchenko abase themselves and seem to invite abuse. Lebedyev in turn tortures those like General Ivolgin who are weaker than himself. The passionate nature of the underground man can be seen in Ippolit's violent changes of mood; his secretiveness and brooding melancholy are illustrated by the portrait of Rogozhin.

DOSTOYEVSKY AS PSYCHOLOGIST

Dostoyevsky's extraordinary psychological insight has been acclaimed by many critics, some of whom have gone so far as to call him the "father of psychology." The comparisons which have frequently been made between the Russian author and Shakespeare in this respect are not unjust. We must remember, however, that the term "psychologist" as applied to Dostoyevsky must be interpreted in a highly literary sense. He makes no attempt to classify or analyze psychological types. His characters have their origins as the embodiments of ideas; they are not completely rounded people. They are creations of the writer's art, not case histories, and as such they are dramatically more interesting and convincing within the framework of the novel than a "real" person could be. This kind of characterization is one of the things that makes Dostoyevsky a Romantic rather than a Realist novelist. In accordance with his dramatic method, Dostoyevsky makes the ideas and motivations of his characters clear by their actions and the interplay with other characters. The important figures in *The Idiot* are all psychologically complex. For example, although psychologists recognize the split personality which is portrayed in Dostoyevsky's "doubles" as a form of schizophrenia, they would never, as the author does in the case of Myshkin and Rogozhin, consider two people as halves of a single personality. The Russian author's interest in dreams and their interpretation foreshadows the Freudian principle of dream-interpretation as a guide to the subconscious.

SYMBOLISM IN THE IDIOT

Symbols are not of the first importance in *The Idiot*; Dostoyevsky uses them incidentally and unconsciously to a degree. As we might expect, the symbol of the cross is connected with Prince Myshkin. He and Rogozhin exchange crosses, an act which ordinarily is a declaration of brotherhood, but which here reminds us of the strange relationship of the two as complementary parts of a single soul. Myshkin also buys a cross at an inflated price from a soldier. Dostoyevsky is saying here that some Russians have sunk so low that they will sell Christ, as Judas did, while he also makes clear that Myshkin, as Christ, cannot refuse the Cross which is the symbol of suffering and redemption. The repeated reference to Holbein's painting of the "Descent from the Cross" is a variation of the same theme. The duality of Myshkin and Rogozhin is further emphasized by Rogozhin's symbol, the knife. The knife inexplicably attracts the Prince when he sees it in Rogozhin's room, and he is reminded of it when he sees a similar knife in a shop window (the "sixty-kopek item," as the author mysteriously calls it). There are two reasons for the Prince's fascination with the knife: with its blade and guard, it is described as being cross-shaped; and Myshkin has a premonition that Rogozhin will use it to kill Nastasya.

THE SYMBOLISM OF IPPOLIT'S DREAM

The dream which Ippolit Terentyev describes at such length in his "Essential Explanation" utilizes and clarifies several of the recurrent **themes** employed in the novel. Dostoyevsky habitually uses lower animals - spiders, beetles, cockroaches, flies - to symbolize the evil principle in the world. The tarantula (an especially large spider) in Ippolit's dream is a specific example of this symbol. Rogozhin's appearance in the dream immediately after the spider confirms his position as a manifestation of this evil principle. The "scorpion-like animal" of Ippolit's earlier dream, with its two large feelers just below the head, also has the shape of a knife or distorted cross. Dostoyevsky may also have intended the reader to make a connection between the symbol of the spider and Lebedyev's interpretation of the "Star called Wormwood" from the Biblical book of the Apocalypse as the network of railways which spreads spider-like over Europe. Certainly Dostoyevsky feels that the railways are representative of the harmful Westernizing influence on Russia, with its emphasis on mechanical progress that crushes man's spirit.

SYMBOLISM OF THE FLY

The fly is a recurrent but ambivalent symbol in *The Idiot*. At Pavlovsk, Ippolit complains that even the fly is better off than he, for it knows its place in the sun. The Prince feels a peculiar sympathy and identification with this remark. To Ippolit, the fly is a paradoxical symbol both of union with nature and of separation from it. The idea is brought back with telling force by the buzzing of a fly as the "doubles" keep their bizarre wake over Nastasya's body at the end of the book; at this point the fly is the only living thing in a world of the dead.

DOSTOYEVSKY'S REPUTATION WITH RUSSIAN CRITICS

As we might expect, the attitudes which critics have taken toward Dostoyevsky's novels reflect changing taste and the ascendancy of various schools of critical interpretation from the 1860s to our own time. The "discoverer" of Dostoyevsky, the Russian critic Vissarion Belinski, praised his first novel, *Poor Folk*, for its combination of **realism** and social consciousness. As the writer's style became less realistic and more exclusively concerned with ideas in the later novels, however, Belinski and his contemporaries condemned the loss of "clarity" and Dostoyevsky's growing political conservatism. There followed a vogue for trying to prove that all the circumstances and characters of the novels were based on incidents and associates of Dostoyevsky's own life. The idea of the "double" was apparently too confusing for these early critics. Then for a time after the overthrow of the Tsarist government in 1917, Dostoyevsky was hailed as the man who had correctly predicted the revolution, but was condemned for his attacks on those who contributed to it, the Nihilists and Radicals. Although the author had no intention of writing political novels, Russian criticism of him even today seems unable to keep appraisal of his literary art separate from their distaste for his politics.

DOSTOYEVSKY'S REPUTATION WITH WESTERN CRITICS

It is a tribute to Dostoyevsky's skill as a writer that each new school of critical thought in the West has acclaimed him as a master of its own ideas. He has been hailed as a pioneer worker in the field by the exponents of social **realism**, the psychological novelists, the symbolists, the imagists and the existentialists. What Dostoyevsky himself would have thought of these strange bedfellows makes an interesting question. While there still is no lack of exclusively social, psychological or theological interpretations of the Russian's work, there has been an encouraging trend of late to view the novels as complete works of art. Critics familiar with a broad range of ancient and modern literature have recognized Dostoyevsky's novels for the masterpieces they are, and have made illuminating comparisons between these works and books as diverse as the early Greek *Iliad of Homer* and the novels of the American Henry James. The idea of a literary **genre** has been used as a most effective tool. To see *The Idiot* as drama, for instance, helps enormously in understanding its structure and the total impression we get from it. The most effective kind of criticism is the sort that tries to see the work as a whole. Only if we think of Dostoyevsky as a man who cared passionately about his social, religious and political ideas, but who was first and last an artist, a creator interested in the making of a complete and coherent work, will we be doing the Russian author full justice.

DOSTOYEVSKY'S ACCOMPLISHMENT IN THE IDIOT

The Idiot is not a typical Dostoyevsky novel, if an expression like "typical" has any meaning when applied to a writer as fertile and inventive as Dostoyevsky. The device of the "double" is found fairly frequently, but the author experiments for the first time in *The Idiot* with the idea of splitting the two halves of the "double's" personality apart and depicting them as two different people. *The Idiot* concerns itself with a higher level of society than most of Dostoyevsky's other novels, in which the petty bourgeoisie and submerged city dwellers figure largely. Yet in spite of the ways in which this novel is atypical, *The Idiot* is a product of Dostoyevsky's mature art and must be ranked only a little, if at all, below his masterpieces, *Crime and Punishment* and *The Brothers Karamazov*. What the novelist has accomplished in this work is the depiction, by and large successful, of a totally good hero. Dostoyevsky realized what an extraordinarily difficult task he had undertaken: he himself said that the only successful example was *Don Quixote*. At the same time the novelist has presented a large gallery of characters who are carefully individualized so that together they seem to make up an entire society. We see few sides of their personality, but they are depicted with such skill that we think of them as real people. What Dostoyevsky has achieved in his novel can be described as the supreme goal of the Romantic novelist. He has created a world that is not the real world, and which we know is not real, but which is so intense and so true that after we have read *The Idiot* we never again see the real world with quite the same eyes.

THE IDIOT

. . . .

The questions and discussion given here are only samples of the very large number of questions that can be asked about a novel as complex as *The Idiot*. The discussions simply suggest one possible line of attack in answering the question; almost any number of other approaches can be used. In addition, bear in mind that some of the statements made are necessarily matters of opinion.

Question: The most important point about the character of Prince Myshkin is his resemblance to Christ. What literary advantages does Dostoyevsky gain from this parallel?

Answer: Dostoyevsky's portrayal of Myshkin as a Christ-like figure is done consciously and with a specific purpose in mind. The author deliberately sets himself the very difficult literary task of describing a totally good man because such a portrait is essential to the ideas which he wants to advance in the novel. The Russian writer wishes to show the decadence, the moral and spiritual decay of Russia in his own day. To do this he puts a simple, transparently honest creature, the Prince, right in the middle of this maelstrom of self-seeking and corruption. The strong contrast between Myshkin's behavior and that of all the people around him helps Dostoyevsky make his point.

Once he has established the parallel between Christ and Prince Myshkin, the author is in a position to reap a number of advantages. For example, as soon as the reader is aware that Myshkin is Christ-like, most of the work of characterization is done at a single stroke. People know what Christ was like and how he reacted on various occasions; we can simply assume that the Prince will react in the same way. The author is free to concentrate on the details of his hero's personality - the broad outlines are already filled in. At the same time, Dostoyevsky puts the importance of his **theme** beyond question. No fictional work which has a Christ-like man for a hero can possibly turn into a vulgar comedy or a mere society novel. The reader knows that Christ had a mission on earth, and he immediately assumes that the Prince will have one too. The tension which is built up as we try to figure out what this mission is keeps the reader's attention firmly fixed. Another advantage is the continuous **irony** provided by the fact that the Prince is the representative of Christ, but is considered an "idiot" by most of those around him. The title, "The Idiot," with its overtones of child-like simplicity, is a stroke of genius on Dostoyevsky's part. We see the author, in the older **connotations** of the word, touching on the **theme** of the mad but divinely inspired prophet. The wandering Russian holy man, insane by any ordinary standards but in close communion with God, was still a familiar sight in nineteenth-century Russia, and Prince Myshkin has some of the characteristics of this figure.

We can see, then, that the author profits in a number of ways by making his hero into a Christ-figure. He simplifies characterization, establishes the importance of his **theme**, and provides dramatic tension. A number of modern novelists have done the same thing for many of the same reasons. One example, perhaps less successful than Dostoyevsky's, is Ernest Hemingway's last novel, *The Old Man and the Sea*. There are, of course, also dangers in this sort of portrayal. For one thing, no matter how good or wise he is, the hero of the novel always falls short of our conception of Christ; he can never be more than an imitation. For specific purposes, however, such as Dostoyevsky's desire to advance a serious and important **theme**, the Christ-figure as a literary device is exceedingly useful.

Question: *The Idiot* has been called a Romantic novel. Do you agree with this description?

Answer: If we define the goal of the Romantic novelist as the creation of a private world where he, the author, sets the rules so that he can achieve a particular effect or advance a specific idea, then Dostoyevsky is such a novelist. The microcosm of St. Petersburg society which he shows us is like no "real" world we have ever seen, and the incidents and behavior of the characters are unbelievable from any "practical" point of view. Yet while we are reading the book we do not question the authenticity of the Russian author's creation, but accept it completely. This statement is another way of saying that *The Idiot* is a successful Romantic novel, and a successful work of art.

We can see *The Idiot* as a Romantic novel more clearly if we look at the things omitted that a realistic or "naturalistic" novel would include. None of the characters in *The Idiot* seems to worry about making a living. We never see them at work; in fact, they all have infinite amounts of time in which to meet, discuss each others' personalities, quarrel, engage in courtship, and tell tall tales. For the same reason there is little or no description of scenery; we know no more about how the Russian countryside looks when we finish the novel than before we began it. We are also shown no more than a narrow segment of society. The middle class predominates, with no peasants and very few real aristocrats appearing. All these limitations make up the boundaries of Dostoyevsky's highly personal world of *The Idiot*. The life of the novel is in the personalities of its characters, and if we are to follow his rules we must look no further. If we enjoy the book at all, we do not even want to.

Question: What are some of the flaws in *The Idiot* as a work of literature?

Answer: *The Idiot* demonstrates some of the difficulties associated with writing for serial publication and in great haste, as Dostoyevsky did. Under the circumstances (he finished the long first part of the novel in just over three weeks) it is remarkable that the story is as coherent and free from inconsistencies as it is. Occasionally the author forgets a fact: Prince Myshkin is told, on at least two and possibly three occasions, that Nastasya is writing to Aglaia, and each time he expresses great surprise and disbelief. A more serious inconsistency is that of character. General Epanchin is shown as a rather mean, sensual man in the first part of the novel, and as a kindly, doting (though stupid) father in the last half. Rogozhin is obviously meant to represent evil in a heroic way; he should be demonic, but as the book progresses he descends to the level of the magician in a tale of the supernatural, whose eyes glow at us from dark corners. The young nihilists, too, are meant to be thoroughly bad, but Dostoyevsky only succeeds in showing them as rather stupid, aimless young men, and Ippolit finally ends by inspiring our sympathy. There are minor anomalies even in Myshkin's character. We are never sure whether his love for Aglaia is simple human attraction to a beautiful woman, or a variation on the pity he extends to Nastasya. If he really loves Aglaia and intends to marry her, why does he say twice previously that his illness makes marriage impossible for him?

In his attempt to write a novel of ideas, Dostoyevsky does not always succeed in integrating his ideas into the story. Some of the long philosophical harangues in which Prince Myshkin and Ippolit engage interrupt the plot and make dull reading besides. The author is at his best when his thoughts are illustrated naturally by a discussion between the characters.

The last objection to be made concerns the multiplication of characters. Ideally, every figure in a novel should have some indispensable part in the plot, some essential, if small, task to perform. There are many characters in *The Idiot* who appear once and drop out of sight; they could be eliminated with advantage. Even a person as relatively important as Ferdyshtchenko has no connection with the **theme** of the book. His presence is only confusing, and his functions could easily be divided between Lebedyev and General Ivolgin. As for more minor characters, such as Lieutenant Kurmyshov, who challenges the Prince in the park at Pavlovsk; Doktorenko, Lebedyev's nihilist nephew; and the whole cast of aristocrats at the Epanchin's "engagement party," they add nothing but background noise when we are straining to hear the words of the play.

Question: Is the form of *The Idiot* **epic** or dramatic?

Answer: *The Idiot* is definitely dramatic in form. The **epic**, which employs the narrative technique, usually progresses on a more or less level plane until it rises to a single **climax**. A dramatic work (which does not, of course, have to be a play) can be divided into a series of important episodes, each of which has a definite beginning and end. Often these **episodes** end with a minor **climax**, and the major climax occurs near the close of the work. (The technical name for the **climax** of a tragic work is the **catastrophe**, a word originally applied to the Greek tragic dramas and now extended to cover all tragedies.)

This episodic pattern, which helps to identify a dramatic work, can be found in *The Idiot*. The pace of the novel rises to a feverish pitch in a number of climactic "scenes," in which the main characters are involved and which mark an important stage in the story. These scenes, when they are isolated from the rest of the novel, can be seen as dramatic in themselves. That is, the confrontations between the characters, the exits and entrances, and the dialogue, are all managed just as they are on the stage. Information is conveyed almost exclusively through dialogue; what little description there is takes the form of stage directions.

Dostoyevsky's dramatic technique can be illustrated by an examination of one of these "scenes," in this case a relatively minor one: Prince Myshkin's first visit to the Ivolgin household in St. Petersburg. It can be found in Part I of *The Idiot*, Chapters 8 through 11. The author has carefully prepared us for these events. The Prince has a logical reason for going home with Ganya; he has nowhere to stay in Petersburg, and wants to rent a room. The fact that his family has to rent out rooms to make a living reminds Ganya of their poverty, and he becomes tense and angry. From the moment of their entrance the atmosphere is explosive.

The apartment is described in detail, with the position of all the rooms and an account of the furniture and other decorations (stage directions). Ganya's mother and his sister Varya are then introduced, together with his young brother Kolya. We see at once that they contrast strongly with Ganya in appearance and temperament, and this difference adds to the emotional tension of the scene.

Comic relief is now provided by the entrance of the obsequious Ferdyshtchenko. His appearance is outlandish, and almost his first act is to warn Prince Myshkin not to lend him money. He is immediately followed by General Ivolgin, whose shabby-genteel dress at once proclaims his character. The General proceeds to act out a melodramatic reunion scene based upon the idea, entirely a product of his imagination, that he had known the Prince's parents and the Prince himself as an infant. Naturally enough, Myshkin is mystified by all this.

The action now moves to the drawing room, where discussion arises over Nastasya's portrait. The picture is a standard device of nineteenth-century melodrama. It gives the actors something to gesture at while they strike tragic attitudes. As Varya and her mother are discussing the picture, Ganya re-enters the room and becomes furiously angry with Myshkin for showing them the Portrait, though he is actually quite innocent. Just as the argument over Ganya's fiancée (Nastasya) is at its height, the Prince notices someone standing at the door and opens it. It is Nastasya. The trick of having someone come on the stage just as the other actors are quarreling furiously over her picture has enormous dramatic impact. As a stage device this technique is not exactly subtle, but it is effective. The **irony** of the situation is heightened by the fact that Nastasya mistakes Prince Myshkin for a servant, and insists that he announce her. As a result, the Prince must walk into the middle of the quarrel in the drawing room and say loudly, "Nastasya Filippovna!" These words end the chapter. No better example of Dostoyevsky's cliff-hanging technique could be desired. Ending the chapter is, of course, equivalent to dropping the curtain. The author tells us (at the beginning of the next chapter) that dead silence follows this announcement, but the information is entirely unnecessary. We know that everyone in the room has been struck dumb.

Ganya, who is already very disturbed, is both dumbfounded and embarrassed by this new visitor; and when Myshkin tells him rather abruptly to stop staring, Ganya nearly attacks him. Crowd scenes and tableaux are among Dostoyevsky's strong points as a writer, and this scene, with Ganya and Myshkin confronting each other in the middle of the room, while the rest of the family and Nastaya look on, is one of the best of them. The tension is finally broken by Ganya, who tries to relieve his embarrassment by presenting the Prince as a new and entertaining curiosity on the Petersburg scene. The General enters, on his best behavior, and proceeds to tell Nastasya the story of an incident which happened to him. She cruelly points out that she read exactly the same story a few days before in a Belgian newspaper. The tension has built up again, and Nastasya's hysterical laughter and the General's humiliation are interrupted by a loud ring at the bell. Rogozhin has arrived. While his entrance does not have quite the magnificent stage management of Nastasya's, he soon gains the spotlight by audaciously trying to buy Ganya off and offering Nastasya a huge sum of money in cash. The tension rises higher and higher; Ganya's sister Varya insults Nastasya, and Ganya raises his arm to strike her. Myshkin intercepts him and Ganya, enraged, slaps him in the face. We have reached another melodramatic high point. The slap shows Ganya's lack of self-control and his cowardly tendency to take out his anger on those who are really only bystanders, like the Prince. It also makes an important point about the Prince's character. In Russia at the time, an insult such as this would inevitably have resulted in a duel, but Myshkin, following one of the most basic precepts of Christianity, literally "turns the other cheek." The slap marks the climax of the whole **episode**, and like a good playwright, Dostoyevsky hurries all his characters off the stage to avoid an anti-climax.

The development of the whole affair is brilliant. In a characteristic way which is almost unmatched in literature,

Dostoyevsky piles incident upon incident, each more melodramatic and outrageous than the last. At the exact point that the reader's sense of credibility will tolerate no more, he breaks off the action and finishes the scene. The use of the dramatic method here enables Dostoyevsky to focus on the area in which he is primarily interested, the characters and the interaction between them. This interplay of characters determines the plot, not vice versa. In addition he can build suspense superbly when he treats the **episode** as a scene in a play; the successive entrances have all the impact they would have on the stage. In fact, Dostoyevsky convinces us that for the kind of novel he is writing, the dramatic method is the only possible one to use.

Ardalion Alexandrovitch Ivolgin: A retired general, he spends most of his time drinking and telling fantastic stories, and pays little attention to his family.

Gavril Ardalionovitch Ivolgin (Ganya): General Ivolgin's eldest son. He is secretary to General Epanchin but hopes to better his social position by marrying either Aglaia Epanchin or Nastasya.

Nikolay Ardalionovitch Ivolgin (Kolya): Ganya's teenage brother. He is friendly and helpful to everyone, especially to Prince Myshkin.

Nina Alexandrovna Ivolgin: General Ivolgin's long-suffering wife.

Varvara Ardalionovna Ivolgin (Varya): Sister to Ganya and Kolya. She marries Ivan Ptitsyn.

Katya: Nastasya's maid.

Keller: A retired army lieutenant and ex-boxer. He is uncouth but loyal to Prince Myshkin.

Kurmyshov: A lieutenant in the army and a friend of Radomsky.

Lukyan Timofeyevitch Lebedyev: A minor official who ingratiates himself with anyone possessing wealth or power. He is first attracted to Rogozhin, and then to Myshkin.

Vera Lukyanovna Lebedyev: Eldest of Lebedyev's four children. The sweetness of her disposition contrasts with her father's malice.

Prince Lyov Nokolayevitch Myshkin: An idealistic young man who has been incapacitated by epilepsy most of his life. He is the "idiot" of *The Idiot*.

Nikolay Andreyevitch Pavlishtchev: Prince Myshkin's benefactor. He does not appear in the novel, having died before it begins, but is referred to frequently.

Ivan Petrovitch Ptitsyn: A rather successful money-lender whom marries Varvara Ivolgin.

Yevgeny Pavlovitch Radomsky: An army officer. Aglaia refuses his proposal of marriage.

Parfyon Semyonovitch Rogozhin: A young man of lower middle-class origins who has inherited a fortune. He pursues Nastasya throughout the novel and acts as Prince Myshkin's opposite.

Prince S.: He is engaged to Adelaida Epanchin.

Dr. Schneider: He runs the clinic in Switzerland from which Prince Myshkin came to Russia, and to which he returns.

Ippolit Terentyev: A youth of eighteen who is dying of tuberculosis. He is Kolya Ivolgin's best friend.

Marfa Borissovna Terentyev: Ippolit's mother and General Ivolgin's mistress.

Afansky Ivanovitch Totsky: Nastasya's seducer and protector. At one time he hopes to marry Alexandra Epanchin.

THE IDIOT

Alexey: The Epanchin family's footman.

Bahmutov: A schoolmate of Ippolit Terentyev. He is referred to but does not appear in the novel.

Nastasya Filippovna Barashkov: Initially, Totsky's mistress, but later sought after by Ganya, Myshkin and Rogozhin.

Antip Burdovsky: He claims to be the illegitimate son of Prince Myshkin's benefactor, Pavlishtchev.

Princess Byelekonsky: Madame Epanchin's social patroness.

Darya Alexeyevna: A friend of Nastasya. She is a middle-aged actress with a house in Pavlovsk.

Vladimir Doktorenko: Lebedyev's nephew. He engineers Burdovsky's attempt to swindle Myshkin by pretending to be Pavlishtchev's son.

Adelaida Ivanovna Epanchin: The second of the Epanchin sisters. She is engaged to Prince S.

Aglaia Ivanovna Epanchin: The youngest and most beautiful of the Epanchin sisters. She is proposed to by Gavril Ivolgin, Prince Myshkin and Yevgeny Radomsky.

Alexandra Ivanovna Epanchin: The eldest of the Epanchin girls. At one time it is thought that she may marry Totsky.

Ivan Fyodorovitch Epanchin: He has the rank of a general and is a member of the civil service. Although he indulges in occasional amorous escapades, he is devoted to his wife and daughters.

Lizaveta Prokofyevna Epanchin: Formerly Princess Myshkin, she is distantly related to Prince Myshkin. She spends most of her time worrying about her daughters.

Ferdyshtchenko: A comical, disreputable drunkard who lodges at the Ivolgins'.

Madame Filisov: A friend of Nastasya. She is Lebedyev's sister-in-law. Nastasya stays at her house in St. Petersburg.

Ivan Petrovitch: An "elderly anglomaniac." He is a distant relation of Pavlishtchev.

BIBLIOGRAPHY

....

BIOGRAPHIES AND BOOKS OF CRITICISM

The following bibliography lists books containing material on Dostoyevsky and his works. Most critical works deal with all of Dostoyevsky's major novels, not just *The Idiot*. The books starred are available in paperback.

Berdyaev, Nicholas. * *Dostoevsky*. Translated by Donald Attwater. New York: Meridian, 1957. A concentration on Dostoyevsky's philosophical and religious ideas distinguishes this book. Berdyaev's interpretations are generally sound, although occasionally his own prejudices get the better of him.

Carr, Edward H. * *Dostoevsky: 1821–1881*. New York: Barnes and Noble, 1962. Carr's book is one of the best combinations of biography and critical commentary available. Chapter XV, "The Ethical Ideal-*The Idiot*," provides a balanced discussion of the ideas and literary techniques used in the novel.

Coulson, Jessie. *Dostoyevski: A Self-Portrait*. London: Oxford University Press, 1962. This life of Dostoyevsky is made up of excerpts from his letters and diaries, held together with a small amount of narrative. The Russian author's account of his troubles while writing *The Idiot* is particularly interesting.

Dostoyevsky, Fyodor. *The Diary of a Writer*. Translated by Boris Brasol. New York: Charles Scribner's Sons, 1949. In this diary Dostoyevsky recorded in detail his ideas for new novels, his progress on them, financial matters, and any amount of fascinating trivia. The book is essential for any serious study of the novelist.

Fueloep-Miller, Rene. *Fyodor Dostoevsky: Insight, Faith, and Prophecy*. New York: Charles Scribner's Sons, 1950. The author discusses Dostoyevsky's interest in dreams and the various prophecies that are made in *The Idiot*. The novelist's forecasts of what would happen if Russia did not leave the path of materialism and atheism have proved uncannily correct, but his hope for a religious revival has not been borne out.

Gide, Andre. * *Dostoevsky*. Norfolk, Conn.: New Directions, 1961. This book is an interesting example of a certain kind of criticism, in which the critic uses ideas from his author as a springboard for a discussion of his own philosophy. The book has stimulating ideas, but is far more Gide than Dostoyevsky.

Hingley, Ronald. *The Undiscovered Dostoyevsky*. London: Hamish Hamilton, 1962. The author takes original and provocative points of view towards a number of ideas about Dostoyevsky. For instance, he maintains that the Russian is a comic novelist, perhaps without knowing it.

Hubben, William. * *Dostoevsky, Kierkegaard, Nietzsche, and Kafka*. New York: Collier Books, 1957. The men named in the title are discussed as important thinkers of the nineteenth (and twentieth) centuries, and as providing the groundwork for the philosophy of Existentialism.

Ivanov, Vyacheslav. *Freedom and the Tragic Life: A Study in Dostoevsky*. New York: The Noonday Press, 1952. Ivanov's work contains very sound comments on Dostoyevsky's novels as tragedy, myth and theology. He goes beyond literary "sources" to the universal ideas that underlie the works.

Payne, Robert. *Dostoyevsky: A Human Portrait*. New York: Alfred A. Knopf, 1961. A good, standard biography, Payne's work is based primarily on Dostoyevsky's many letters. Payne finds much autobiographical material in the novels.

Seduro, Vladimir. *Dostoyevski in Russian Literary Criticism*. New York: Columbia University Press, 1957. A detailed examination of critical reaction to Dostoyevsky from his own time to the present day is presented in this scholarly work. It is extremely valuable but specialized, and of interest primarily to the serious student.

Simmons, Ernest J. *Dostoevsky: The Making of a Novelist*. London: Oxford University Press, 1940. Simmons' book is one of the most valuable examinations available of Dostoyevsky's novels as works of literature (rather than as philosophy, psychology, etc.). The critic examines how the novels were written.

Steiner, George. *Tolstoy or Dostoevsky: An Essay in the Old Criticism*. New York: Alfred A. Knopf, 1959. A brilliant examination into the place of Dostoyevsky's (and Tolstoy's) novels among the world's great works of literature, this critical work provides the best analysis of the novelist's dramatic technique.

Yarmolinsky, Avrahm. *Dostoevsky: His Life and Art*. New York: Criterion Books, 1957. This lively and detailed biography by an expert on Russian literature is marred by critical comments on the novels which are over-simplified and obvious. The background material on Russian life in the nineteenth century provides valuable insights into Dostoyevsky's world.

Yermilov, V. *Fyodor Dostoyevsky*. Moscow: Foreign Languages Publishing House, n.d. The Russians, after all, should understand Dostoyevsky best, and this down-to-earth criticism provides a good deal of sound thinking on the novelist and his work. In the field of politics, however, the Marxist ideology takes over, and Dostoyevsky is condemned as a reactionary without any examination into what made him that way.

HISTORIES OF RUSSIAN LITERATURE

These works can be useful when more detailed books of criticism are unavailable. The entries on Dostoyevsky are necessarily short and compressed.

Mirsky, D.S. * *A History of Russian Literature.* New York: Vintage Books, 1958. The section on Dostoyevsky in this book gives a very useful brief analysis of the novelist's thought, and general criticism of the novels as a group, primarily from a literary point of view.

Muchnic, Helen. * *An Introduction to Russian Literature.* New York: E. P. Dutton and Co., 1964. As its title implies, this book is intended as a basic introduction for the new student, but the comments on Dostoyevsky's novels are unusually sensible and helpful.

Slonim, Marc. *The **Epic** of Russian Literature: From Its Origins Through Tolstoy.* New York: Oxford University Press, 1950. Slonim's work is a full-dress history of Russian writing, and the chapters on Dostoyevsky are long and attempt to present most of the important critical information on the novels. Short summaries of the major novels are also provided.

ESSAYS AND ARTICLES IN PERIODICALS

Many of these essays and articles deal directly with *The Idiot.* The others deal with specialized aspects of Dostoyevsky's ideas and literary techniques which are of particular importance in the novel.

Blackmur, Richard P. "*The Idiot:* A Rage of Goodness," in *Eleven Essays in the European Novel.* New York: Harcourt, Brace and World, 1964. Blackmur is one of the outstanding critics of our time, and his essay provides brilliant philosophical and literary insights into the ideas of *The Idiot*. The style of the essay is compressed and difficult; no allowance is made for the less experienced reader.

Chamberlin, William H. "Dostoyevsky: Prophet and Psychologist." *Russian Review*, Volume VII, Number 2, 1948, pp. 34–40. This article provides an interesting analysis of Dostoyevsky's ideas and beliefs in relation to the facts of the author's life; Chamberlin feels that the novels are intensely subjective.

Krieger, Murray. "Dostoyevsky's *Idiot:* The Curse of Saintliness," in *Dostoevsky: A Collection of Critical Essays*, edited by Rene Wellek. Englewood Cliffs, N.J.: Prentice Hall, Inc., 1962. Wellek's book contains one of the best and most sophisticated collections of essays on Dostoyevsky obtainable. Almost every important issue is examined in the book. Krieger's article is an intriguing comparison of *The Idiot* with Pierre by the American novelist Herman Melville. It suffers somewhat from Krieger's attempt to force Prince Myshkin into the mold of the tragic visionary.

Lesser, Simon D. "Saint and Sinner: Dostoyevsky's *Idiot*." *Modern Fiction Studies*, Volume IV, Number 3, 1958, pp. 211–224. *The Idiot* is examined in this study from an almost exclusively psychological point of view. The article provides a good example of the usefulness of psychological analysis in depth. It also shows the limitations of investigation from a single point of view.

Matlaw, Ralph E. "Recurrent **Imagery** in Dostoyevsky," *Harvard Slavic Studies*, Volume III, 1957, pp. 201–225 (for *The Idiot*, especially pages 212–216). An exhaustive analysis of Dostoyevsky's **imagery** and symbolism is provided here. The article clarifies a number of puzzling points about Dostoyevsky's always unspecific and unclear use of symbols.

Mortimer, Ruth. "Dostoyevsky and the Dream." *Modern Philology*, Volume LIV, 1957, pp. 106–116. A good general commentary is provided on the use which Dostoyevsky makes of dreams in his novels. Little specific attention is paid to *The Idiot*.

Poggioli, Renato. Chapter II. "Dostoevsky: on Reality and Myth," in *The Phoenix and the Spider*. Cambridge, Mass.: Harvard University Press, 1957. This is a highly interesting but very "advanced" and theoretical piece of literary criticism which uses all the latest terminology. In its attempt to see the novels as "pure literature," it provides an antidote to the surfeit of psychological and philosophical analyses.

Strom, George G. "The Moral World of Dostoyevsky." *Russian Review*, Volume XVI, Number 3, pp. 15–26. Strom's article is just what its title implies, a moral, and not primarily literary, examination of Dostoyevsky's work. It is particularly useful because it attempts to relate the character of Prince Myshkin to the basic principles of Christian philosophy and mysticism.

Tate, Allen. "The Hovering Fly," in *On the Limits of Poetry: Selected Essays, 1928–48*. New York: Swallow Press, 1948. Tate uses the fly which appears in the last scene of *The Idiot* as the point of departure for an examination of actuality and the nature of poetry. The essay tends to be abstruse, but is stimulating and suggestive.

Traversi, Derek A. "Dostoevsky," in *Dostoevsky: A Collection of Critical Essays*, edited by Rene Wellek. Englewood Cliffs, N. J.: Prentice Hall, Inc., 1962. This far-ranging essay is an attempt to explain Dostoyevsky's exploitation of the senses and Prince Myshkin's "mysticism." Traversi's arguments are daring, controversial, and thought-provoking.

THE IDIOT

Themes of *The Brothers Karamazov* Dostoyevsky and Social Criticism *The Brothers Karamazov* and Modern Society The Nature of Guilt in *The Brothers Karamazov* The Nature of Suffering in *The Brothers Karamazov* Dostoyevsky's Theory of Punishment Religion and Atheism in *The Brothers Karamazov* Sensuality as an Alienation Technique Ivan Karamazov and the Supremacy of Reason Dostoyevsky's Philosophy of History Dostoyevsky and the Myth of Progress

TOPICS FOR PAPERS

1. What is true freedom for Dostoyevsky?

2. Compare Alyosha with Prince Myshkin in *The Idiot*.

3. Read *Brave New World* and compare it to the ideas in "The Legend of the Grand Inquisitor."

4. What is the concept of freedom in *Notes from Underground* and "The Legend"?

5. The **theme** of rebellion in Schiller and Dostoyevsky.

6. Compare Kafka's and Dostoyevsky's view of the human condition.

7. What role do the boys play in the novel?

8. Some readers consider Rakitin more repulsive a figure than Fyodor. If this is so, why?

9. In what way does Katerina torture Dmitri with her love?

10. Hatred and love as the novel's unifying principle.

11. What are the different ways in which myth appears in the novel?

12. In what ways are Kolya Krassotkin and Ivan similar?

13. How does the Grand Inquisitor define freedom and happiness?

14. According to the Inquisitor, in what way did Jesus ask too much of mankind?

15. Why does the Grand Inquisitor say that Christianity is a practical impossibility?

COMPARISON WITH OTHER WRITERS

Dostoyevsky's impact on twentieth-century literature is well-nigh incalculable. A comparison of his work with the following selected authors would be particularly worthwhile.

Gerhart Hauptmann Theodore Dreiser Marcel Proust Franz Werfel Andrei Gide D.H. Lawrence George Orwell Franz Kafka Thomas Mann Hermann Hesse William Faulkner Aldous Huxley Albert Camus Jean Paul Sartre

PRONUNCIATION OF PRINCIPAL CHARACTERS' NAMES

The transliteration of Russian names into English is phonetic. Depending upon the translation, the author's name is spelled Dostoyevsky, Dostoevsky, Dostoievsky, or Dostoievskij. There is no correct English spelling as such. The Russians pronounce it: dus-TOY-evsky.

Middle names in Russian are patronymics, derived from the first name of the person's father. Thus, all the children of one family will bear the same patronymic. The masculine and feminine forms vary slightly.

Alyosha (Alyosha). The youngest and most religious son of Fyodor.

Dmitri (Dmeetree). Fyodor's eldest son. Hotblooded and passionate.

Fetyukovich (Fyetyukovich). Dmitri's lawyer.

Fyodor (Fyodor). The father of the four sons.

Grigory (Grigoree). Family servant.

Grushenka (Grooshenka). The object of Fyodor's and Dmitri's passion.

Ilusha (Eelyusha). Captain Snegiryov's son. Dies of consumption.

Ivan (Eevan). Fyodor's intellectual son.

Katerina Ivanovna (Kahtyereena Eevahnuvna). The woman who wants to marry Dmitri.

Kolya Krassotkin (Koly a Krasotkin). The precocious leader of the schoolboys.

Miusov (Mewsoff.) The superficial liberal.

Rakitin (Rahkeeteen). A novice and unprincipled opportunist at the monastery.

Smerdyakov (Smyerdyakof). Fyodor's illegitimate son.

Snegiryov, Capt. (Snyegeeryof). Father of Ilyusha.

Zossima (Zosseemah). The Elder of the monastery.

CHRONOLOGICAL TABLE OF DOSTOYEVSKY'S MAIN WORKS

1846 *Poor Folk, The Double, The Landlady, White Nights.*

1858 *Uncle's Dream.*

1859 *The Village Stepanchikovo*

1861–62 *The Insulted and Injured, Notes from the House of the Dead.*

1863 *Winter Notes on Summer Impressions.*

1864 *Notes from Underground.*

1865 *Crime and Punishment.*

1866 *The Gambler.*

1868 *The Idiot.*

1870 *The Eternal Husband*

1871–72 *The Possessed*

1873 *A Gentle Creature, First installments of The Diary of a Writer.*

1875 *A Raw Youth.*

1880 *The Brothers Karamazov.*